Making Your Dreams Your Destiny

A Woman's Guide to Awakening Your Passions and Fulfilling Your Purpose

MAKING YOUR DREAMS YOUR DESTINY

JUDY RUSHFELDT

CASTLE QUAY BOOKS
CANADA

Making Your Dreams Your Destiny: A Woman's Guide to Awakening Your Passions and Fulfilling Your Purpose

Copyright ©2005 Judy Rushfeldt
All rights reserved
Printed in Canada
International Standard Book Number: 1-894860-33-0

Published by: Castle Quay Books
500 Trillium Drive, Kitchener, Ontario, N2G 4Y4
Tel: (800) 265-6397   Fax (519) 748-9835
E-mail: info@castlequaybooks.com
www.castlequaybooks.com

Copy editing by Audrey Dorsch, Dorsch Editorial
Cover Design by John Cowie, *eyetoeye design*
Printed at Essence Publishing, Belleville, Ontario

All Scripture quotations, unless otherwise marked, are from *The Holy Bible, New International Version*. Copyright © 1973, 1978, 1984. International Bible Society. Used by permission of Zondervan Publishing House. All rights reserved. • Scripture quotations marked KJV are from *The Holy Bible, King James Version*. Copyright © 1977, 1984. Thomas Nelson Inc., Publishers. • Scripture quotations marked NKJV are taken from the New King James Version. Copyright © 1979, 1980, 1982. Thomas Nelson Inc., Publishers. • Scripture quotations marked AMP are taken from *The Amplified Bible*, Old Testament. Copyright © 1965, 1987. Zondervan Corporation. *The Amplified New Testament*. Copyright © 1954, 1958, 1987. Lockman Foundation. Used by permission. • Scripture taken from *The Message*, copyright © by Eugene H. Peterson, 1993, 1994, 1995. Used by permission of NavPress Publishing Group.

Library and Archives Canada Cataloguing in Publication

Rushfeldt, Judy, 1955-
    Making your dreams your destiny : a woman's guide to awakening your passions and fulfilling your purpose / Judy Rushfeldt.

Includes bibliographical references and index.
ISBN 1-894860-33-0

    1. Women--Psychology. 2. Self-actualization (Psychology)
3. Self-actualization (Psychology)--Religious aspects--Christianity.
I. Title.

BF637.S4R85 2004   158.1'082   C2004-905419-8

To my husband Brian,
for encouraging me to pursue my dreams

Table of Contents

1. THE MESSAGE OF THE BOXES. 11

Boxes and Boundaries 13

The Benefits of Life in a Box 17

The Price of Life in a Box 18

Your Gifts, Talents, and Resources 19

2. DARING TO DREAM 25

God: The Greatest Dreamer of All 26

Permission to Dream. 29

Your Dreaming Muscles 32

3. YOUR SPIRITUAL BIRTHRIGHT 35

Conception of Purpose 36

Dormant Purpose. 39

Restored Purpose. 40

4. THE NURTURED HEART 47

The Wellspring of Life 48

Heart Toxins 49

Heart Nutrients. 51

5. THE RESTORED HEART 63

The Wounded Heart. 66

Purified Passions 71
The Tested Heart 75
The Valued Heart. 78

6. EMBRACING CHANGE 81
Shed the Old. 83
Step Out of Your Comfort Zone 86
Embrace the New 89

7. UNFOLDING VISION. 93
Progressive Revelation. 94
Faithfulness 96
The Next Step. 99
Testing the Vision 101
The Process. 104

8. DISCERNING YOUR PASSIONS. 107
Unveiling Your Passions 110
Identifying Your Passions. 112
Trying Something New 114

9. DEFINING MISSION, VISION, AND GOALS. . . . 119
Your Personal Mission Statement 121
Your Vision Statement. 125
Your Action Plan 127

10. DREAM THIEVES. 135
The Mockers. 136
The Inner Critics 140
Character Compromise 143
Mediocrity 146

11. CONQUERING FEAR 151
Fear: A Robber. 153
Love: The Foundation of Courage. 156
Facing Your Fears 159
Building Your Courage Muscles 164

12. RUN TO WIN 167

    Run Lightly. 168

    Run with Focus 169

    Run with Discipline 171

    Run with Endurance 173

    Help the Runner Next to You 176

    Run with Faith 178

    Run with Peace 182

    Remember the Reason for the Race. 184

Notes 189

Peace with God. 195

Chapter One

The Message of the Boxes

> *Two roads diverged in a wood*
> *and I took the one less travelled by,*
> *and that has made all the difference.*

Robert Frost, *The Road Not Taken*

One morning about fifteen years ago, I was rummaging through some old boxes packed away in a forgotten corner of my basement when I discovered a stack of poems I had written during my childhood. Shaking off the dust and cobwebs that clung to the thin, yellowing paper, I began reading.

I discovered a long-forgotten world—one that sang with romance, adventure, and mystery. It was a world of princesses, heroes, and castles, where the princess was always rescued and the dragon always slain. Each flower had a name; children flew on magic carpets; and a pot of gold glittered at the end of every rainbow.

I felt an aching sense of loss. A part of me was packed away with those poems, neatly mummified in coffins of mediocrity. Somewhere along the way, my world had begun to shrink from one that sang with unlimited possibilities to one that conformed to narrow, predictable boundaries.

For years, I was haunted by a persistent inner nagging that I had only scratched the surface of my potential. Though I had developed some gifts and pioneered a few challenging endeavours, there were vast reservoirs of potential I had never dared explore.

A *Peanuts* comic strip depicts Charlie Brown's dog, Snoopy, struggling to balance a doghouse on his back. The caption reads, "There's nothing heavier than the burden of potential."

That's exactly how I felt—weighed down by the oppressive burden of unrealized potential. Somewhere along the way, dream thieves had skulked into my heart and captured the inner visionary, locking it up as a prisoner of war and slowly starving it until all that remained was a lifeless skeleton.

For years, I was haunted by a persistent inner nagging that I had only scratched the surface of my potential. Though I had developed some gifts and pioneered a few challenging endeavours, there were vast reservoirs of potential I had never dared explore.

Most of us become prey to dream thieves at one time or another. They infiltrate our hearts through failure and heartache, setbacks and tragedy, criticism, and pressure to conform to the status quo. Not every story has a happy ending. Dragons rip out our hearts and even laugh while we bleed. At the end of some rainbows are pots of despair. Pain and disappointment visit us all, some of us more frequently and fiercely.

Dream thieves will mock you from without and taunt you from within. Some are disguised in the cloaks of duty and drudgery, convincing you that it is irresponsible to pursue your passions.

Others are disguised as shame and self-condemnation, cloaking fears, unhealed emotional wounds, and a history of failures.

Many dream thieves require no disguise; they brashly swagger through the wide-open door of mediocrity that many of us allow to pervade our lives.

Finally, in my thirties, I decided I was no longer willing to be stifled in a self-imposed box. I made a commitment to evict the dream thieves and release the inner visionary from captivity. The time had come to re-envision my future in light of Jesus' words, "With God all things are possible."[1]

Once I made that decision, I was launched on an adventure of discovery, transformation, and growth. At times, the path led to mountaintops of joy; at others, it twisted through dark and barren valleys of discouragement. But along the way, my inner dreamer slowly woke from slumber, shook off the grave clothes, and learned to dance again.

Somewhere along the way, dream thieves had skulked into my heart and captured the inner visionary, locking it up as a prisoner of war and slowly starving it until all that remained was a lifeless skeleton.

What about you? Do you have a passion that grips your heart, that won't let you go? Do you have a clear sense of purpose for your life? Are you living your dream?

Or have the dream thieves robbed you of your destiny? Have you limited yourself to what you believe is practical? Are you in the habit of filtering your dreams through the lens of other people's expectations and opinions? Have you disengaged from the deepest passions of your heart?

More importantly, are you tired of living in captivity? Are you ready to commit yourself to pursuing the pathway of purpose?

Helen Keller described life as "either a daring adventure or nothing." What would you prefer—a boring, unchallenging life of mediocrity or a passionate adventure in faith?

The path of mediocrity is much easier, of course. Safe and predictable, it's the path of least resistance and the road most travelled.

The pathway of purpose, on the other hand, is often difficult, dangerous, and lonely. You will be challenged to step out of your comfort zone. Fear and doubts will emerge as you break out of your box and dare to pursue your dreams. You may even lose some friendships, as some people will feel threatened by your new-found liberty.

But your life will also change in ways that you never dared imagine! God will liberate your inner dreamer from captivity, ignite vision in your heart, and release you to soar into your destiny.

Boxes and Boundaries

Once upon a time, we were curious, passionate, and thrilled to be alive. The world was our footstool; it offered unlimited possibilities.

We could do anything. We could become anyone we envisioned. Dreaming was as natural as breathing.

Remember when you learned to colour? I especially liked colouring with chalk. What power! The neighbourhood sidewalks were my canvas as I used every colour in my chalk collection to create childish masterpieces. (At least, I thought they were brilliant.) Best of all, no one complained or tried to stop me.

Then I went to kindergarten and learned to colour within the lines.

My colouring book was dotted with red, green, silver, and gold stars, rewarding my conscientious efforts to conform to the boundaries.

But when I thought my teacher wasn't looking, I pulled scraps of paper from my bookbag and created my own drawings, splashing the pages with the princesses and leprechauns that danced through my imagination. Instinctively, I knew I must keep these drawings hidden. One day, enraptured with my make-believe world, I didn't notice the teacher standing over my desk. Furious, she reprimanded me for my misdeed and threw my drawings in the garbage.

I'm sure she meant well. After all, she was only doing her job. Nevertheless, the sad reality is that the "message of the boxes" begins bombarding us in childhood and continues throughout life. Transmitted from many sources, this message steals creativity, paralyzes passions, and traps dreams.

The message of the boxes says, "*It can't be done.*" Nagging you to accept the status quo, it says, "*Your dreams are unrealistic.*" It taunts you about your shortcomings and reminds you of your limitations. It insists the obstacles are too great to overcome.

On a personal level, we may hear the message of the boxes from parents, teachers, friends, relatives, school counsellors, college professors, religious leaders, and others. On a societal level, it is conveyed through the media, education system, social attitudes, and popular culture.

Conformity is a common message that limits many. *Don't be different. Take the safe path. Don't rock the boat. You can't trust your desires. Don't share your uniqueness. Adventure is dangerous. Repress your dreams. Embrace security. Play it safe. Take the road most travelled.* Those who refuse to conform are mocked and ostracized. Eventually, most people succumb to the pressure to colour within the lines, even when everything inside of them cries out to paint a picture that has never before been envisioned.

But as Dale Carnegie has said, "The 'sure thing' boat never gets far from shore."

Other negative messages are communicated through criticism, abuse, or a lack of love and affirmation; these are especially damaging in the vulnerable childhood years. Many children are subjected to a relentless barrage of negative words, attitudes, and behaviours that convey a sense of inability: *You're a failure. You never do anything right. You're stupid. You have no talents. You don't measure up.*

If you were repeatedly criticized and undermined, or never affirmed and encouraged, you may have internalized these critical messages and developed a deep sense of inferiority.

Finally, another common message of the boxes—one that pervades society today—is mediocrity. Rather than exalting the virtues of excellence and hard work, popular culture and the education system encourage people to do just enough to get by. It's far easier to blend in with the mediocrity crowd than to pursue excellence.

These are just a few examples. The message of the boxes comes in many forms and is conveyed through a variety of sources, but the end result is the same—a paradigm of living that is severely limited. Sapping courage and eroding confidence, these messages hinder you from developing your gifts and embracing opportunities. Little by little, you draw boundaries around your attitudes, thoughts, and dreams. Eventually, each area of your life reflects the message of the boxes.

You may become boxed in by other people's opinions, trapped by fearful thoughts, such as *What if I look like a fool? What will people think? What if I fail? If I tell people my dreams, will they laugh?*

The message of the boxes may taunt you from within. Frequently, we are our own worst enemies. Self-doubt, fear, and intimidation encase hopes and dreams in a concrete shroud. Inner critics repeatedly remind us of our faults and failures. These thoughts become loudest and harshest when we begin to step out to pursue our dreams.

Over the years, I have spoken with many friends who have passions and dreams. Some dream of starting their own businesses. Others dream of writing songs, novels, or devotionals. One lady cherishes a dream of becoming an artist. Another has a dream to establish a ministry for inner-city youth. One woman has a vision for an outreach program in her neighbourhood. Some desire to counsel abused women or start an orphanage for unwanted mentally challenged children or a prayer chain for their neighbours or co-workers. Others have secret yearnings to run for political office.

Their faces radiate passion and joy as they share these cherished longings.

Though some of these women have gone on to pursue their dreams, the sad reality is that most have not. Their secret yearnings remain trapped by the message of the boxes.

Many people are afraid to even dare imagine what their lives might become if they were to break out of their boxes. Some have lived in a box for so long that they're not sure they want to venture into a place with no boundaries. After all, life in a box is familiar, safe, and predictable.

Yet every so often, a tiny flame of hope flickers in their heart; for brief moments they wonder, *Is this all there is? Why was I born? Isn't there more to life than this? What on earth am I here for?*

I've lived both inside and outside of a box. I've known the frustration of suffocating in a box of intimidation and doubt; I've also known the joy of breaking free and living my dreams. Once I began to soar above my limitations and embrace my dreams, my only regret was that I didn't venture out of my comfort zone sooner.

What about you? Does your life reflect your deepest values and passions? Does it ring true with the person you really are, deep in your heart?

Or do you feel an inner restlessness that is often symptomatic of a lack of authenticity, of not being true to your heart? Perhaps you feel as though you are living according to the blueprints of others, rather than honouring your core values and deepest sense of calling.

Is your creativity stunted, repressed by fear or self-doubt? Have areas of your life become stagnant? Are you frustrated? Are you easily intimidated? All these are symptoms of living beneath your divine purpose.

Many people try to anaesthetize these feelings with busyness and materialism. They attempt to drown out the quiet inner voice of purpose by filling their lives with the loud and tyrannical voice of the urgent. Yet even amid the constant noise and activity, the yearning for purpose refuses to release its grip.

Imagine, for a moment, how different your life might be if you broke free of your box and followed the desires of your heart. Imagine the possibilities if you were unencumbered by fear, intimidation, and self-doubt. What would you do? Would you change occupations? Is there something you yearn to do—something that burns in your heart that you have never shared with anyone?

The first step to breaking out of your box and reaching for your dreams is to be honest with yourself. Stop pretending that everything is fine. Resist the temptation to silence the inner voice that cries out for purpose by filling your life with meaningless activity and clutter.

I suggest you take a couple of hours alone, away from your busy schedule, and think about why you have remained in a box. First evaluate the benefits of life in a box; then consider the price.

The Benefits of Life in a Box

You may be thinking, *What possible benefits could there be to living in a box?* Well, none, of course. But there certainly are *perceived* benefits; otherwise, why would so many people live there?

One perceived benefit, for example, is predictability. Uncomfortable with change, many people like the security of a predictable life, regardless of the price they may be paying in boredom and frustration.

Protection from failure might be another perceived benefit. People who dare to think outside of the box and dream big are popular targets for criticism from the mediocrity crowd. Boxes are shields against criticism.

Another perceived benefit might be protection from failure. Life outside of the box is undeniably high risk. The more you step out to try something new, the greater you risk failing and looking foolish in the eyes of others. This haunting fear of

> *The first step to breaking out of your box and reaching for your dreams is to be honest with yourself. Stop pretending that everything is fine. Resist the temptation to silence the inner voice that cries out for purpose by filling your life with meaningless activity and clutter.*

failure keeps many people from venturing out of their boxes.

Finally, there is protection from emotional pain. When you tap into your heart's desires and step out to pursue your dreams, fears and unresolved emotional issues often surface—and these must be dealt with.

Be brutally honest as you search your heart about why you have accepted the boxes.

The Price of Life in a Box

Now evaluate the price you are paying to live in a box.

This will take some honest soul-searching, especially if you are in the habit of repressing your dreams and desires. You may have ingrained habits of living according to what you feel you *should* do, rather than ordering your life in harmony with your deepest values and sense of calling. You may be so enslaved by other people's opinions that you have not allowed yourself to consider the price you are paying for life in a box.

You may be paying the price with anger, resentment, and a lack of energy or motivation.

You may be paying the price with boredom and frustration, knowing deep in your heart that you were born for something much greater than what you are experiencing.

You may be paying in your relationship with God. Deep down you know that he has called you to develop your gifts and passions, but your dreams remain frozen in glaciers of fear.

Finally, you may be paying with agonizing regrets over wasted potential and missed opportunities.

Now weigh the benefits of living in a box against the price you are paying.

Prayerfully evaluate the choices you have made. Mark out the direction you are heading. Ask yourself if you are truly living with purpose. Compare the benefits and price of life in a box.

Ask yourself, *Are the so-called benefits worth the price I am paying?* More importantly, *Am I willing to let go of the counterfeit protection afforded by living in a box to embrace my dreams and purpose?* My prayer is that you will answer no to the first question and yes to the second. Decide today to begin the journey of breaking free of your box to embrace your dreams.

Your Gifts, Talents, and Resources

"A rock pile ceases to be a rock pile the moment a single man contemplates it, bearing within him the image of a cathedral," wrote Antoine de Saint-Exupéry in *Flight to Arras*.

What do you see when you consider the raw materials—the talents, spiritual gifts, time, and opportunities—that God has given you? A rock pile? A cathedral? More importantly, what have you done with these resources? If you were to give an account today of how you have developed your raw materials, what would you say? Would God be pleased?

In the parable of the five talents, Jesus illustrates the importance of developing and stewarding our abilities and resources.[2] A businessman entrusted differing amounts of wealth, called "talents," to three servants to manage while he went away on a long journey. (A talent of gold was equivalent to about $29,000 or twenty years' wages.) When he returned, he asked each servant to account for what he had done with the money.

The two individuals who had received five talents and three talents received great rewards. By wisely investing the money, they had doubled its value. Their work was crowned with success.

Similarly, when we faithfully steward the resources God has entrusted to us, our efforts are also crowned with success. The principle of multiplication goes into effect; our gifts and talents become more effective.

> *"A rock pile ceases to be a rock pile the moment a single man contemplates it, bearing within him the image of a cathedral,"* wrote Antoine de Saint-Exupéry in Flight to Arras.

The third man in this parable missed out on the rewards of success, for he chose the comfortable and risk-free path of mediocrity. Choosing to bury his talent, he made no attempt to develop, improve, or invest it. Treasuring safety and security over growth and pleasing God, he did what far too many people do with their gifts and resources—absolutely nothing.

What this man failed to realize is that he never owned the talent in the first place. A steward is one entrusted with the responsibility of managing another person's property. Unconcerned about the prospect of one day giving an account to the owner, this man justified his inaction with the excuse "I was afraid."

Why was he so afraid? Perhaps he compared himself with those who received more talents and buried his out of intimidation. Perhaps he feared that he would fail and look bad in other people's eyes. Perhaps he was just plain lazy, lacking a sense of accountability to his master.

One of the first steps to breaking out of our boxes is to realize that we do not own our gifts and talents; God does, and he expects us to do our very best to invest them in serving God and other people.

I can think of many occasions when I held back from using a gift because I had fallen into the trap of comparing myself with others who were more talented. When I compared myself with others, intimidation followed. I responded by withdrawing and hiding my gift rather than risking rejection.

Over the years, I've learned to appreciate the wisdom in Henry Van Dyke's words, "The woods would be silent if no birds sang except those that sang best."

Fear may influence us to bury our gifts and shrink from pursuing opportunities. But, as in the parable of the talents, fear is no excuse, for God promises that he will empower us to develop the gifts he has entrusted to us.

The number of talents we receive is not the issue, nor is the magnitude of the talent. The one and only issue is what we do with what we have received. In far too many lives, gifts are buried or squandered.

In the graveyard where my baby brother Steven is buried (he was stillborn, never having a chance to develop his potential), inscriptions on the other gravestones indicate that most were blessed with long lives. I wonder how many of these people accomplished their life destinies. How many others were buried with unrealized potential—books that were never written, songs that were never sung, love that was never shared, words that were never spoken, ventures that were never risked?

You have an absolutely unique constellation of gifts and talents that you were meant to share with this world. Don't rob the world by taking your dreams to the grave with you. Don't let the years pass by and reach the end of your life suffering agonizing regret as you look back and see nothing but unrealized potential.

"Twenty years from now you will be more disappointed by the things that you didn't do than by the ones you did do," said Mark Twain. "So throw off the bowlines. Sail away from the safe harbor. Catch the trade winds in your sails. Explore. Dream. Discover."

What you are is God's gift to you. What you do with yourself is your gift to God and the world!

Many of the world's greatest geniuses died without ever succeeding at anything. Why? It takes more than talent and good intentions to be successful. It takes boldness and faith. Most of all, it takes a deep commitment to faithfully steward the gifts, time, and opportunities God provides for each one of us.

Accepting responsibility for stewarding your dreams and resources can feel threatening, especially at first. As you take an honest look at how you have developed your potential, no doubt you'll realize—like me and like most people—that you have made some less-than-ideal choices. Perhaps you have wasted time. Perhaps you have pursued materialism over purpose, worldly success over destiny, or the accolades of others over the approval of God. Perhaps you have succumbed to fear, people-pleasing, or just plain laziness.

Don't waste more time by beating yourself up with self-condemnation. Trust in the Bible's promise: "And we know that in all things God works for the good of those who love him."[3]

The moment we commit to pursuing the path of destiny, God takes the good, bad, and ugly parts of our lives and weaves them together into a tapestry of beauty and purpose.

The past is behind you, but the future is before you! The choices you make today will define your future.

"It must be borne in mind that the tragedy of life doesn't lie in not reaching your goal," said Benjamin E. Mayes. "The tragedy lies in having no goal to reach. It isn't a calamity to die with dreams unfulfilled, but it is a calamity not to dream."

Some people feel as though it's too late. Some feel they have wasted too much time or too many opportunities. Some feel they are too damaged, too dysfunctional. Some feel they are simply too old.

21

Golda Meir may have felt that way before she decided to run for political office, but she didn't let that stop her. She was seventy-one years old when she was elected prime minister of Israel.

"It must be borne in mind that the tragedy of life doesn't lie in not reaching your goal," said Benjamin E. Mayes. *"The tragedy lies in having no goal to reach. It isn't a calamity to die with dreams unfulfilled, but it is a calamity not to dream."*

Grandma Moses may have felt she was getting a bit of a late start when she launched her painting career at the age of seventy-six. Arthritis had made it difficult for her to hold the needles for doing embroidery and needlework, so she took up painting. Grandma Moses especially enjoyed painting simple scenes of farm life. Before long she won national recognition, with her paintings widely reproduced through prints, greeting cards, and magazines. At the age of one hundred she illustrated "'Twas the Night before Christmas" by Clement Moore (1962).

I know a gentleman in his seventies who recently completed law school. After retiring at the age of sixty-five, he became bored and frustrated. He began to pray that God would give him something meaningful to do in his later years. Soon his heart began to burn with a vision to defend religious freedoms in the courts. Most people, when reaching this age, wind down. This visionary, however, embarked on the most challenging and rewarding season of his life.

A friend in her fifties is taking her first writing course, finally pursuing a passion she has cherished since childhood. Another friend, whom I have known since childhood, now in her forties, has just joined a singing group—something she has always longed to do but never had the confidence to pursue until now. Others are going back to college or starting new businesses or pioneering new ministries.

Middle age challenges us to evaluate what we have accomplished with our lives. It is a time of reckoning—of realizing that life without purpose is no life at all. Many people make radical occupational changes not only in their forties and fifties but also into their sixties, seventies, and even later.

For many women, middle age is also a time of transition when children are leaving home to start their own careers and families.

Having focused their talents and energy on the noblest profession of all—motherhood—they reach a stage where their children are grown and they are ready to enter the next season of life.

One friend, who just turned forty-five, describes this season as her "second adolescence." Though she treasured the years of parenting, her children are grown. In the past two years she has explored various avenues of creativity and just recorded her first CD.

Age is not a factor. Talent is not a factor. Intelligence is not a factor. Real or perceived emotional limitations are not factors. Money is not a factor. The one and only factor is whether or not you are willing to make a decision—starting today—that you will commit yourself to the journey of discovering and fulfilling your potential.

When a young eaglet reaches a certain level of maturity, the mother eagle must help him learn to fly. Because the eaglet wants to stay in the nest and be fed, he won't take the initiative to leave the nest. But an eagle is not created to sit in a nest; he is destined to soar through the skies and enjoy great heights.

This doesn't just happen, though. The mother eagle has to prod the eaglet into his destiny. The way she does this is to knock him out of the nest and let him fall. When he falls far enough, she catches him on her wings. She keeps repeating the process until the eaglet learns to spread his own wings and fly.

Like the young eaglet, we humans tend to prefer the comfort and security of our nests to the risks of charting new territory and flying to new heights. But we were never designed to stagnate in nests of mediocrity—we were created for faith and adventure.

When I sensed God beckoning me to step out of my comfort zone and envision my future based on Jesus' words, "With God all things are possible," a whole new world of possibilities and opportunities opened to me. I discovered for myself the reality of the Bible's promise that God is truly able to do "immeasurably more than all we ask or imagine, according to his power that is at work within us."[4]

If you yearn to step out in faith and embrace all that God has for you, get ready for the most exciting journey of your life. Get ready for God to knock you out of your nest. Most importantly, get ready for the excitement of learning to fly and the joy of soaring into vast new horizons of purpose and potential.

For Personal Reflection or Group Discussion

1. Is there an area of your life where you feel boxed in? Describe how it has affected you.

2. What is the main source of the "message of the boxes" in your life (e.g., childhood experiences, criticism from others, pressure to accept the status quo)?

3. What is the main reason you have stayed in your box? Do you fear failure? Are you afraid of stepping out of your comfort zone?

4. Do you long for greater purpose? Are you ready to start re-envisioning your future in light of Jesus' words, "With God all things are possible"?

Chapter Two

Daring to Dream

*The future belongs to those who believe
in the beauty of their dreams.*

Eleanor Roosevelt

If you were to embark on a search for the world's most passionate visionaries, where would you look? In the executive boardrooms of Fortune 500 companies? At a convention of motivational speakers? In a laboratory of the world's top scientists researching a cure for cancer?

Though I'm sure those places are swarming with visionaries, there's an even better place to search. And it's much closer than you might think.

Just visit your local playground. Ask a group of five-year-olds what they want to be when they grow up and they'll say things like, "I want to be . . . a fireman . . . an author . . . a lawyer . . . a world traveller . . . the first female president of the United States or prime minister of Canada . . . a mom . . . an artist . . . a missionary . . . a foster parent . . . a pilot . . . an evangelist . . . the founder of an orphanage . . . the president of the world's biggest company . . ."

Watch how their eyes sparkle with enthusiasm as they share their dreams. Their attitude seems to say, "I can do anything. The opportunities are endless. The world is my footstool."

Ask a group of adults to share their dreams, and the responses will be decidedly different. Some might stare at you with a glazed expression, as though they didn't understand the question. You'll probably hear many responses like "I don't know" or "What do you mean?" or "I wouldn't mind a better job" or "I want to be financially independent" or "I want my kids to get into an Ivy League college" or "I want to win the lottery" or "I want to retire" or "I want a bigger house."

In all likelihood, very few would passionately and confidently share a dream that burns in their heart.

Dreaming is natural for most children, for life has not yet hardened their hearts. They remain attuned to that visionary trait that God carves into the soul of every human being. But somewhere along the sojourn from childhood to adulthood we disengage from our hearts and lose touch with our passions. Dreams that once burned brightly dim to a barely discernible glimmer. Some have been snuffed out altogether.

In the real world of competitive job markets, family responsibilities, and concerns about financial security, dreaming seems impractical, even irresponsible. The very word conjures memories of the second-grade teacher yelling, "Stop daydreaming and get to work!" the parent who nagged, "Come off cloud nine," or the condemning inner voices that scold, *Dreaming is selfish, wasteful, and foolish.*

God: The Greatest Dreamer of All

The Bible says we were created in God's image.[1] It also encourages us to cultivate that image by pursuing ongoing spiritual growth.

In light of that, perhaps one of the most important questions we could ever ask is, What is God really like?

When I consider this question, the theological part of me stands to attention and reiterates, "God is holy, merciful, just, loving, righteous, kind, gracious, all knowing, faithful, all powerful," and so forth.

But another part of me cries out that these terms merely scratch the surface in describing my Creator.

I grew up in one of the most beautiful places in the world, the Columbia Valley, nestled between the Rocky and Selkirk mountain ranges in western Canada. Though I've travelled to many countries around the world, I still consider this little piece of paradise one of the most spectacular anywhere. I have my own name for this area— the Valley of Dreams.

When I need to be reminded of my heavenly Father's awesome creativity and majesty, I visit the Valley of Dreams. Even in the midst of some of the darkest seasons of my life—when dreams had died and hope had dissolved into despair—even then, a tiny part of my soul would begin to sing again.

Sometimes the miracle of renewed hope dawned in my heart as I watched the moon dancing on snow-capped mountain peaks. Sometimes it happened as I listened to the wind playing with the aspen leaves, strumming songs of mystery and promise and new beginnings. Often, hope ignited in my heart as I watched the glory of a Rocky Mountain sunrise, celebrated by the chorus of a thousand robins, blue jays, and meadowlarks.

Over the years, my Valley of Dreams has opened my heart to the artistic, creative, adventurous, even romantic facets of God—traits that could never be comprehended by theology alone, any more than the beauty of a rainbow can be grasped through a scientific dissertation about light refractions and dust particles.

The Bible confirms that God reveals dimensions of his character through nature, telling us that his divine power and divine nature "have been clearly seen, being understood from what has been made."[2] The Psalmist proclaimed, "The heavens declare the glory of God; the skies proclaim the work of his hands."[3]

Consider the scope of imagination involved in creating 10,000 species of frogs, 250,000 species of flowers, and 300,000 species of beetles. Consider the creative genius reflected in each snowflake— one cubic foot of snow contains eighteen million snowflakes, yet the pattern of each is absolutely unique. Consider the universe, with millions of galaxies loaded with billions of stars.

Open the eyes of your soul, and you will see the face of the Creator mirrored everywhere. As the poet William Blake wrote in his *Letter to Dr. Trusler*, "The tree which moves some to tears of joy is in the eyes of others only a green thing that stands in the way. Some see nature all ridicule and deformity . . . and some scarce see nature at all. But to the eyes of the man of imagination, nature is imagination itself."

Every dimension of the natural creation sings of the majestic creativity of our heavenly Father.

There's something even more amazing: the greatest expression of divine creativity is not seen in nature—but in us! The Bible says that humanity is crowned with "glory and honor."[4]

Look at our physical bodies. Scientists are amazed by the incredible complexity of the thousands of separate but interconnected systems within the human body. As the editors of *ABC's of the Human Body* wrote,

> The most incredible creation in the universe is you—with your fantastic senses and strengths, your ingenious defense systems, and mental capabilities so great you can never use them to the fullest. Your body is a structural masterpiece more amazing than science fiction.[5]

And all of this doesn't even begin to explore the complex and mysterious wonders of the human soul. Think about it—you and I represent the greatest investment of God's creative imagination! Not only do we embody the ultimate expression of God's creative genius, we are also partakers of that same creative nature. Divine creativity is irrevocably imprinted on our souls.

Regrettably, the divine image was marred by independence from God. Creativity—like all the divine characteristics—was flawed by our fallen nature, sin, and separation from God.

That's the bad news. The good news is that the moment we choose to reunite with God through Jesus Christ, God breathes his own spirit into us.*

The Bible says, "Therefore, if anyone is in Christ, he is a new creation; the old has gone, the new has come!"[6] Not only does God place his Spirit in us, he begins to transform our character the instant we are spiritually reborn, recreating the divine characteristics that were marred by sin. One of those divine characteristics is visionary creativity.

---

* If you are interested in understanding more about knowing God personally, see "Peace with God" following the Notes at the back of this book.

Permission to Dream

Hopefully by now you are convinced that God is a dreamer. So, give yourself permission to dream! The Bible encourages us to develop a more Christlike character.[7] That means not only striving to become more loving, kind, selfless, and holy—it also means becoming more of a visionary.

Visionaries are creative, imaginative, and resourceful. Possibility thinkers, they continually aspire to grow in faith and believe in God's power and ability to work through them to achieve great feats for his glory.

"You are a child of God—your playing small does not serve the world," said Nelson Mandela in his 1994 inaugural speech. "There is nothing enlightened about shrinking so that other people won't feel insecure around you. We were born to manifest the glory that is within us. And as we let our light shine we unconsciously give other people permission to do the same."

Some people believe that only a small percentage of the population is born with visionary qualities. It's true that some individuals are exceptionally gifted visionaries. Nevertheless, *everyone* has the God-given capacity to dream. Each of us was born with the innate potential to envision and achieve great things.

You were designed to be a visionary. You were formed to be a conduit of God's glory, power, creativity, and love.

Someone e-mailed me a picture of a kitten staring at the image reflected in a mirror, but the image he saw in the mirror was not that of a tiny kitten. Gazing back at him was a massive, powerful lion, emanating strength, confidence, and courage.

This picture reminded me of the Bible verse, "I can do everything through him who gives me strength."[8]

You may feel small and weak, intimidated by others and by the world around you, but God sees what you can become through faith in him: a person with unlimited potential. Stop seeing yourself through the lens of personal limitations. See yourself through the lens of faith, envisioning what God is able to do in and through you.

Our very humanity cries out to fulfill a unique purpose. With no purpose, we are like fish out of water. Spiritually, we suffocate, for it's impossible to thrive outside of the environment for which we were created. Beauty and creativity are stifled; we live far beneath our potential.

In the book *Man's Search for Meaning*, Viktor Frankl wrote that maintaining a sense of purpose—having a life of meaning—was the one thing that kept some from perishing in Nazi concentration camps. (Frankl survived not just one but four concentration camps.)

With no purpose, the core of our identity shrivels and dies. Eventually, we become frustrated and discontent. We anaesthetize those feelings by filling our lives with busyness and materialism, but a gnawing emptiness surfaces from time to time, reminding us that though we live, we are not truly alive.

Jesus underscored the importance of living with purpose. When his disciples implored him to eat, he responded that his food "is to do the will of him who sent me and to finish his work."[9] It's not that Jesus didn't eat—he did. But his deepest satisfaction came not from food or temporal pleasures. He found joy in fulfilling his purpose.

Jesus had the greatest of dreams: to reconcile humanity to a relationship with God. He never lost sight of that dream and was even willing to be tortured and crucified to see that dream fulfilled.

"Deep in our hearts, we all want to find and fulfill a purpose bigger than ourselves," says Os Guinness. "Only such a larger purpose can inspire us to heights we could never reach on our own. For each of us, the real purpose is personal and passionate: to know what we are here to do and why."[10]

With no purpose, the core of our identity shrivels and dies. Eventually, we become frustrated and discontent. We anaesthetize those feelings by filling our lives with busyness and materialism, but a gnawing emptiness surfaces from time to time, reminding us that though we live, we are not truly alive.

The drive for purpose is so deeply ingrained that it will even seek expression outside of relationship with God.

Every great invention, every painting or musical composition, every child's fingerpainting splattered on the wall, every flair for artistic flower arrangements or love of beauty and romance, every warrior instinct to protect and defend loved ones, every entrepreneurial drive to start new business ventures, every creative act, from a toddler building a sandcastle to an architect designing the world's tallest skyscraper—all these emanate from the divine creativity that is irrevocably stamped on our souls.

Those who have not yet made peace with God may still achieve measures of success, for every creative pursuit stems from the divine image—albeit marred—in the human soul.

We all possess creativity, whether we realize it or not. Even if you have repressed your creative drive, it will find ways to emerge, whether in the impulse to redecorate your home, start a new business, volunteer for a new ministry, or apply creative parenting techniques.

You can't exorcise creativity; it is as much a part of your humanity as your ability to feel joy or sorrow. You can, however, repress it, and if you continue reading this book, you will learn how to tap into and release your divine creativity.

Each of us has been given unique traits and gifts to express beauty where there is ugliness, to bring love where there is hate, to impart colour where there is drabness, and to inspire joy and hope in those trapped by cynicism and despair.

"Purpose is the engine that powers our lives," said Denis Waitley in his book, *Seeds of Purpose*. To serve others and make this world a better place, we must discover our purpose—the unique work that God has called each of us to do. We must stop living in mediocrity. We must rekindle our inner visionary and commit ourselves to the passionate pursuit of purpose.

It is not optional. When we repress vision and creativity, we reject our divine purpose.

God encourages us to connect with our desires and dreams as we rejoice in him. The Bible says, "Delight yourself in the LORD and he will give you the desires of your heart."[11]

Ask God to open your heart to a greater vision of your life. Decide now that you are going to stop listening to the voices of guilt, tradition, negativity, and mediocrity that try to make you feel as though it is selfish or impractical to dream. Listen instead to the gentle whisper of the Holy Spirit beckoning you to come out of your cocoon and become more like Christ—to dream big, expand your boundaries, break out of your box, and become the woman or man you were destined to be.

Your Dreaming Muscles

It's one thing to give yourself permission to dream. It's another to actually do it. Like anything else in life, it probably won't happen unless you make it a priority in your schedule.

In my early twenties I made a New Year's resolution to join a fitness club and participate in aerobics classes three times a week. I hadn't exercised regularly since high school. I showed up for the first class bursting with enthusiasm, determined to give it everything I had. Five minutes into the class, my muscles cramped so painfully I had to quit. Nothing was wrong with my muscles; they were simply weak and atrophied from years of disuse. I modified my goals, starting with five minutes of exercise for the first couple of weeks and gradually increasing the time until I could handle the forty-five-minute aerobic routine. By then my muscles were strong enough to handle the exertion.

If you have never taken the time to dream and explore your passions, you can be sure your dreaming muscles will have atrophied. Perhaps you've never given yourself permission to dream. Perhaps you once nurtured dreams but let them die after years of being assaulted by fear, setbacks, and discouragement.

You've likely heard about the "boiled frog syndrome." If you drop a frog into hot water, it will immediately recognize the dramatic change in temperature and jump out. However, if you place the frog in a pot of cold water and gradually increase the temperature, it will not notice the small but increasing difference. Gradually, it will boil to death.

Dreaming "muscles" don't atrophy overnight. One little adversity after another, a critical word now and then, one setback here, another there—and one day, you realize you have stopped dreaming. The passion is gone. Your heart feels dead. You're just going through the motions.

The good news is you have *not* lost the capacity to dream. True, your dreaming muscles have atrophied through years of disuse, but they *can* grow strong again. As you commit yourself to flexing your dreaming muscles, you will find it progressively easier to think outside of the box. Before long, you will glimpse a vision of purpose and destiny that you never before imagined.

To flex your dreaming muscles, schedule time on a regular basis to dream and let your imagination go. Preface these times with prayer. Choose a peaceful environment. It may be your own living room. It may be a quiet place in nature that nurtures your soul and inspires hope. Even your favourite local coffee shop may help get the creative juices flowing.

Get out several pieces of paper or your journal or your computer and ask yourself, *What stirs my creativity and makes me feel more alive? What makes me feel, **This is what I was born to do?*** Answering the questions at the end of this chapter will help you work through this process.

I suggest you set aside a half-hour a week for this exercise. Imagine you are a child with a box of crayons and a blank piece of paper. Sketch to your heart's content. Use colours that appeal to you.

Write down everything that comes to mind, including anything that may seem ridiculous, crazy, and out of this world. Dream with abandon. At this stage, don't analyze, judge, or hold back. Avoid filtering your thoughts through judgments about what you consider practical or possible. Refuse self-condemning or fearful thoughts such as, *I could never do that. I'm not talented enough. I don't have enough money. I don't have the time. There's no way that could ever happen.*

Let your heart go. Don't edit or censor your thoughts.

Refuse to be inhibited by thoughts like, *What will people think? Am I being silly? Am I being arrogant or unrealistic?*

Avoid worrying about whether your dreams are feasible. Determine to have fun while you develop your dreaming muscles.

Also, do not try to analyze whether these ideas reflect God's will for you. At this stage, you are not committing yourself to a plan of action. All you're doing is cultivating a new habit of thinking outside of the box while you flex your dreaming muscles.

Later we will discuss biblical principles for discerning whether specific dreams or passions harmonize with God's purpose for you. For now, your one and only goal is to flex your dreaming muscles. There's no time like the present—get started now!

For Personal Reflection or Group Discussion

1. Is there something you would love to do so much that you would do it regardless of whether you were paid or anyone else noticed? What is it?

2. If time, money, skills, and circumstances were not obstacles, what would you do?

3. What stirs your creativity and makes you feel passionate and alive?

4. Is there anything that makes you feel, *This is what I was born to do?*

Chapter Three

Your Spiritual Birthright

This dream will challenge, prod, and haunt you until you surrender to its call.

Wayne Cordeiro, *The Dream Releasers*

Teenage girls around the world plaster pictures of him on their bedroom walls. Photographers hound him, shoving each other out of the way to capture his best angle. Journalists speculate about every girl he dates. Royalty watchers gush about his potential to herald a new dawn of dignity for the monarchy.

Prince William is undeniably handsome, talented, and charming. But these qualities are not the main attraction, though they have certainly captivated the public imagination. What enthralls the world most about this young man is his royal destiny as heir to the throne of England, next in line to his father. Prince William's royal title was not something he could earn or buy. Nor was it based on his intelligence, good looks, talents, or achievements. The young prince's destiny was based on the time-honoured tradition of birthright; it was a *fait accompli* before he was born.

You also have a birthright. What's more, your birthright has far greater potential than Prince William's. It has nothing to do with your birth order, race, colour, gender, wealth, or social status. It has nothing to do with your parents, upbringing, looks, IQ, or natural talents.

Just as Prince William's birthright was a *fait accompli* before he was born—before he spoke one word or walked one step or attained one achievement—your spiritual birthright, representing your life purpose, was also destined before you were born, planned in the heart of your heavenly Father. And just like Prince William, you can't earn it, buy it, or deserve it—you can only receive it and walk in it.

But that's where the comparisons end, for Prince William's royal birthright is nothing compared to the spiritual birthright of a child of God. The spiritual riches and destiny awaiting you are far more exciting and glorious than anything granted to earthly royalty. As the Bible says, "We are heirs—heirs of God and co-heirs with Christ."[1]

In light of this amazing spiritual heritage, why do so many of us live as spiritual paupers? Why do some people fulfill their potential while others do not? And, most important, how can we reclaim the spiritual birthright God planned for us before we were born?

Conception of Purpose

The miracle of conception occurs when a father's sperm fuses with a mother's egg to form a single fertilized cell with its own unique genetic blueprint. The new cell splits into two identical cells, then continues to divide and redivide as it travels down the Fallopian tube until it reaches the uterus. After implantation on the uterine wall, the cells rapidly multiply until you have a whole, perfectly formed child. By the time the baby is born, she or he will have sixty trillion cells.

A child's unique genetic blueprint is created at the moment of conception, specifying characteristics such as the colour of the eyes, the texture of the hair, the size and shape of the bone structure, and how tall she will be as an adult. Scientists have also identified genes that affect personality traits and temperament.

Did you know that before you were born, God wove a unique "spiritual DNA" into the fabric of your being? This is your spiritual birthright, representing the purpose God planned for your life. Scientists will never see this DNA under a microscope, for it is spiritual, not physical, but it is no less real.

Just as your physical genetic code is unique, so is your purpose. Even if you have a similar talent or gift to someone else's, it will be expressed uniquely through your personality, life message, experiences, and passions.

There is a psalm that says,

> For you created my inmost being; you knit me together in my mother's womb. I praise you because I am fearfully and wonderfully made . . . . All the days ordained for me were written in your book before one of them came to be.[2]

The same God who designed the splendours of the universe personally planned every little detail about you, including your physical characteristics, personality, talents, and—most important—your life purpose. He never planned for you to live in misery and failure; he planned for you to live with joy and purpose.

God says, "For I know the plans I have for you . . . plans to prosper you and not to harm you, plans to give you hope and a future."[3]

A newly conceived embryo contains the complete genetic code required to mature into a full-term baby, but for that baby to grow she must be nurtured in the nourishing environment of her mother's womb. Similarly, the seeds of purpose require the right spiritual environment to germinate, grow, and blossom.

The first and most important step to ensuring a fertile spiritual environment is to have a relationship with God through Jesus Christ.

Jesus said if we are not abiding in him, intimately connected with him, we are like branches that have been cut off from a vine. The spiritual part of us withers and dies. Because God designed us for relationship with him, our potential can never develop if we are disconnected from our spiritual source.[4]

Jesus also explained how to enter into this relationship when he said, "You must be born again."[5] He was talking about a spiritual birth. When we receive Jesus Christ as our Saviour and Lord, our spirits are awakened to the knowledge of God. His Spirit fills us; from that moment forward, we are able to experience intimate communion with God. Rather than just knowing about God or believing in the existence of God, we truly *know* him in our newly born spirits. As the New Testament says, "The Spirit himself testifies with our spirit that we are God's children."[6]

The moment you are united with God through Jesus Christ, a twofold miracle occurs. First, you become a child of God, with all the rights and privileges of a royal son or daughter. Second, your life purpose is "conceived" by the Holy Spirit. Previously dormant seeds of purpose are connected with the spiritual fountain of life that nourishes their growth. Now God's preordained purpose for your life has the potential to unfold, whereas before it was stunted and dormant.

As you continue growing in your relationship with Jesus Christ, the brand new spiritual embryo (representing your divine purpose) is incubated and nourished. Eventually it blossoms into its full potential. Jesus said, "I am the vine; you are the branches. If a man remains in me and I in him, he will bear much fruit; apart from me you can do nothing."[7]

You may be thinking, *What do you mean we can't do anything apart from Christ? I know lots of successful people who are not Christians.*

Well, there's life. And then there's the rich, full, joyful, purpose-filled life that God desires for each one of us. Jesus also said, "I have come that they may have life, and that they may have it more abundantly."[8] You may achieve measures of outward success without God, but those successes pale in comparison to the treasures of knowing God and the possibilities that unfold to those whose lives harmonize with divine purpose.

Imagine a rose garden that has been neglected for many years. Though the roses are wild and overrun by thorns, some beauty remains. Even so, that beauty can't compare with the glory that can unfold under the care of a skilled gardener.

Sure, you can grow a few roses outside of relationship with God. After all, even when separated from God, we still bear remnants of the divine nature in our souls (though these traits are distorted by sin).

Now imagine the potential of surrendering your life to the loving care of the skilled Master Gardener. Once you experience his touch on your life, you realize that nothing you could ever do on your own compares with what he can do in and through you.

The Bible explains how purpose is released through relationship with Jesus Christ:

For we are God's [own] handiwork (His workmanship), recreated in Christ Jesus, [born anew] that we may do those good works which God predestined (planned beforehand) for us [taking paths which He prepared ahead of time], that we should walk in them.[9]

Dormant Purpose

Your "spiritual DNA"—representing your divine purpose—can never be destroyed. Though it may remain dormant your entire life, it can never be extinguished. The apostle Paul says, "For God's gifts and His call are irrevocable. [He never withdraws them when once they are given.]"[10]

Think about it—other people, circumstances, tragedies, and even your own failures and bad choices can never destroy God's dream for your life! Seeds of purpose are indestructible.

They can, however, remain dormant. There are many reasons for this. One is lack of knowledge. Many people simply don't realize that God has a special purpose for their lives. As Scripture also says, "Where there is no vision [no redemptive revelation of God], the people perish."[11]

Others never reach their potential for they insist on "doing it my way," trying to reach their potential independently of God. Since God made you, it's impossible to truly know your potential or fulfill your purpose outside of relationship with him.

Another reason many people live below their spiritual birthright is that they are crippled by inner brokenness. Having been afflicted by tragedy, rejection, abuse, or other adversities, they find it difficult to believe in a loving and faithful God. Or, if they once had a vision of divine purpose, they stopped believing in their dreams. To embrace a vision of purpose, they need spiritual healing and restoration (see Chapter 5, *The Restored Heart*).

Finally, many people have succumbed to cynicism, having lost the childlike ability to dream. Disconnected from their innermost desires and sense of purpose, they no longer believe in miracles. Cynicism clouds their vision, and they are blinded to the romance and miracle of life.

Restored Purpose

Is it too late for the cynics? Is it too late for those who have lost the capacity to dream? Is it too late for those whose hearts are too crippled by fears to believe their future could have purpose and meaning?

Never. Right up until the moment we breathe our last breath, the seeds of heavenly dreams remain in our hearts, waiting for the right environmental conditions to germinate and blossom. Regardless of how old we are, how many mistakes we have made, how far we have strayed from God, or how many years we have neglected our gifts and talents—it's never too late.

God specializes in restoring dormant purpose and resurrecting dead dreams. One of the words the Bible frequently uses to describe Jesus Christ is *Redeemer*. The Bible is rich with promises of redemption provided through Jesus Christ.

What is redemption? The original Greek and Hebrew words from which the terms *redeem* and *redemption* are translated mean "to buy back." In biblical times, these terms described the cultural practice of paying a full ransom to free a slave or to gain back property that had been taken.

As our Redeemer, Jesus paid the price with his own life to set us free from slavery to inner prisons of sin and brokenness. Not only that, he also paid the price to redeem lost property; that "property" represents your spiritual birthright or destiny.

Though God cannot change your past, he can create beauty out of the ashes of sin, disappointment, tragedy, and failure—releasing purpose into every area of your life.

A few blocks from our home, a natural park extends over 1200 acres. I love to walk there in the early mornings before I begin my day, communing with God and enjoying his creation. A couple of years ago a grassfire burned through a large section in the area I usually walk. Blackened grass was all that remained of the gorgeous array of wildflowers, rosebushes, and aspen and pine trees.

When spring arrived, I was intrigued by nature's miracle of renewal. First, a blanket of grass covered the area. Several weeks later, a few brave wildflowers poked through the surface. As spring progressed into summer, hundreds of varieties of wildflowers, bushes, and trees dotted the area. Soon, the entire landscape blossomed into a magnificent showcase of colour and beauty.

Regardless of how old we are, how many mistakes we have made, how far we have strayed from God, or how many years we have neglected our gifts and talents—it's never too late.

A similar miracle of renewal occurs in us as we grow in our relationship with God. Gifts and potential progressively develop. As they blossom to maturity, they are expressed in a fascinating medley of colours, shapes, and textures through our different personalities, interests, abilities, and life experiences.

Not only can God's power set us free from the bondage of our own sin and negative choices, he can heal the inner wounds inflicted by other people or by painful circumstances. God never wastes anything. He can take the worst things that have happened to you and turn them into something good.

The prophet Isaiah described this wonderful dimension of the redemptive work of Christ in his words,

Surely He has borne our griefs (sicknesses, weaknesses, and distresses) and carried our sorrows and pains [of punishment]. . . . He was wounded for our transgressions, He was bruised for our guilt and iniquities; the chastisement [needful to obtain] peace and well-being for us was upon Him, and with the stripes [that wounded] Him we are healed and made whole.[12]

God is committed to liberating us from bondage into an amazing inheritance as his sons and daughters. We are also reminded that we will be delivered from bondage and "brought into the glorious freedom of the children of God."[13]

Some people seem to have far more opportunities than others to develop their potential. Some seem to have everything going for them—they were raised in loving homes, nurtured in a faith-filled environment, protected from evil influences, and encouraged and affirmed of their value and potential.

Others have experienced the opposite, and much worse. But though these people face gigantic obstacles, God specializes in restoring beauty and dignity to broken hearts and lives.

One of my favourite children's stories is Disney's *Dumbo*. Those of you familiar with the story will remember that Dumbo wasn't always known as the flying elephant. In his early years, he was known as a misfit and was continually ridiculed for his huge, silly, floppy ears.

Needless to say, Dumbo considered his ears a formidable handicap to having friends or achieving happiness.

One day, all of this changed. Along came a little mouse by the name of Timothy. Instead of making fun of Dumbo's ears, he saw their potential. Through Dumbo's bravery and the loyal encouragement of his friend Timothy, Dumbo accomplished the impossible and learned to use his ears to fly. Before long, he became famous all across the land as Dumbo the Flying Elephant.

At one time or another, most of us suffer from what I call "the big-ear syndrome." We look at ourselves and see nothing but flaws. The "big ears" that haunt our lives are different for each of us. They may represent our personality—perhaps we consider ourselves too boring or shy. We may think we have no talent. We may see ourselves as unattractive, unappealing, or unlovable. We may suffer from an overwhelming sense of rejection. We may suffer from emotional scars so painful and debilitating that we are convinced we will never be whole. We may feel misunderstood by others. We may feel too flawed to ever do anything significant. We may be trapped by fears and intimidation. Our potential has been imprisoned by our "big ears"—whatever those represent in our lives.

But just as Timothy looked at Dumbo and saw a very special elephant that was destined to fly, God looks at you and sees all the wonderful things he can do through your life—if you will trust him with your flaws and weaknesses.

There is no such thing as "junk" to God. He views each one of us as having infinite value and potential. His loving eyes see beyond the superficial paint of our outward masks. He looks beyond the nicks and bruises on our hearts and sees the beauty and potential that can unfold under his loving care. And if we are willing to submit ourselves to the Master Potter, he will transform us from the inside out.

God has both the desire and the power to create beauty from the ashes of failure and generate new life from the cesspools of pain and despair. Jesus takes our greatest weaknesses, deepest pains, and darkest shame and applies his healing oil, binds up our wounds, and redeems the wonderful purpose he has cherished in his heart since before we were born.

The very thing you consider your greatest handicap may one day become a key to unlocking your greatest potential. Often it is at the point of our most debilitating weakness that God's power is most powerfully demonstrated. The very thing you fear most may become an area where you experience the greatest measures of what the Bible calls the "anointing."*

I have a friend who suffered repeated sexual abuse as a child. Having experienced inner healing through her relationship with Jesus Christ, she has helped thousands of other sexual abuse survivors find healing through her ministry of speaking, counselling, and writing.

That's the miracle of redemption—God takes the ugly, broken, scarred areas of our lives that we are so embarrassed about and creates a masterpiece of beauty and purpose. It matters not how often or how deeply the arrows have pierced your heart. It matters not how wounded or fragmented your soul is. As your Redeemer, Jesus has his greatest joy in bringing you into wholeness and releasing you to walk in the fullness of your divine purpose.

You may be wondering, *If God planned good purposes for my life, what about all the bad things that have happened to me? What about all the stupid choices I've made and all the wrong turns I took? Did God plan all that?*

---

* The "anointing" of the Holy Spirit is generally understood to represent special supernatural power and authority, enabling a person to fulfill God's purpose. It also refers to God imbuing people with special ability to exercise their gifts with supernatural skill and effectiveness.

No, God did not plan all that. The Bible affirms that God's plans for us are good, but the reality is that we are born into a fallen world. Thus God's divine purposes can be thwarted and delayed by sin, by our own choices, and by Satan, and can be further hindered by the tragedy and pain that is a consequence of living in a fallen world.

But that's not the end of the story. It is merely the context for history's most beautiful story—the victorious message that Jesus Christ paid the price for us to be set free from the repercussions of our sin and bad choices, as well as the scars and brokenness resulting from other people's sins against us.

Erica* exemplifies this miracle of redemption. The product of a violent rape, Erica was conceived on a pile of rotting hay in an abandoned barn. Her mother was so brutally beaten during the rape that she spent two months recovering in a hospital. Though Erica's mother decided to keep her baby, she was never able to love her the same way she loved her other children, who were born later.

Not surprisingly, Erica grew up feeling rejected and flawed. Arrows of shame and self-hatred penetrated deep into the core of her identity. By the time she was fourteen, Erica was taking drugs and having sex with anyone who showed the slightest interest in her.

At seventeen, Erica was befriended by an elderly Christian neighbour. Through loving words and actions, this neighbour began to teach Erica about the love of God. The day finally came when Erica opened her life to Jesus Christ. Over time, she grew to understand her immeasurable worth to God. Though her father was a rapist and her mother rejected her, Erica realized that she was no accident; she was lovingly planned in the heart of her heavenly Father long before she was conceived.

As she continued to grow in her relationship with Jesus, Erica experienced progressively greater freedom from the shackles of rejection and self-hatred. She began to believe the Bible promise that we are "created in Christ Jesus to do good works, which God prepared in advance for us to do."[14]

---

* Name changed to protect privacy.

A dream grew in her heart to found an orphanage that would minister the love of Jesus to abused and abandoned children. Today Erica is doing just that. The very thing that seemed an insurmountable obstacle to happiness God redeemed for a beautiful purpose. The wisdom and empathy Erica learned from having suffered rejection herself now flow through her to bring love and healing to hundreds of heartbroken children.

God's unlimited power and grace are available to each of us to overcome every obstacle that has hindered us from becoming the woman or man he created us to be. Yes, some have to work harder. Some have far more to overcome. But as Jesus said, "My grace is sufficient for you, for my power is made perfect in weakness."[15] The more you have to overcome, the greater your capacity to receive God's enabling grace.

Always remember: you are the only one who can prevent God's dreams from being fulfilled in your life. Many things can lock up our potential, but Jesus has promised to redeem our spiritual birthright and release us into the wonderful purposes he planned for each of us. It starts with a decision. You—and only you—can make the decision that you are tired of the dream thieves that have stolen your spiritual birthright and stunted your potential.

Make the decision today that you will press forward in the journey to embrace your destiny. If you have not done so already, make peace with God. Believe the work Jesus accomplished for you on the cross. Receive him as your own personal Saviour and Lord, and he will forgive your sins and give you a brand new start. He will fill you with his Spirit, create beauty out of the ashes of your life, and empower you to fulfill your purpose.[*]

For Personal Reflection or Discussion

1. What does "spiritual birthright" mean to you?

2. Read Psalm 139:13–16. Can you envision Jesus lovingly weaving

---

[*] If you are interested in understanding more about knowing God personally, see "Peace with God" following the Notes at the back of this book.

you together in your mother's womb? Now read Jeremiah 29:11. God planned *good* for you before you were even born. What impact do these Scriptures have on you?

3. Can you think of areas of your life where your God-given potential has remained dormant and never developed? To what do you attribute this?

4. Recalling the story of Dumbo, do you have an area you consider a handicap to becoming the person you were created to be? Can you think of how God might transform that area of weakness into something that will help you serve others?

Chapter Four

The Nurtured Heart

Above all else, guard your heart,
for it is the wellspring of life.

Proverbs 4:23

P regnant with her first child, Jill* could barely contain her excitement over the hopes and dreams she cherished for her unborn baby, whom she had already named Mara. (She felt sure it was a girl.) She practised the lullabies she would sing as she nursed Mara at her breast. She envisioned how Mara's eyes would light up on Christmas mornings. She dreamed of Mara's first day at school, her first date, and her college graduation. She even imagined how Mara might look in her wedding gown.

Suddenly, on a bleak November morning in the fourth month of her pregnancy, Jill miscarried. Like a sandcastle swept away in high tide, her precious dreams dissolved in a sea of despair. She eventually learned that a normally harmless medication prescribed by her doctor had produced an allergic reaction that triggered the miscarriage. Though Jill later gave birth to three healthy children, she never stopped grieving for Mara.

---

* Name changed to protect privacy.

Jill's anguish is incomprehensible to those of us who have never lost a child. Equally incomprehensible is the grief our heavenly Father must feel when the dreams he cherishes for his beloved children never reach fruition. Considering the wealth of potential residing in each of us, his heart must agonize over gifts that are never developed, callings that are never embraced, and destinies that are never fulfilled.

Think about the joy and pride you feel when your own children develop their talents and achieve success. God also feels joy and pride—only much more so, for his love for us is far greater than any human love. He yearns to see his children become all we were created to be.

Although it's true that God has a purpose for your life, it's also true that that purpose doesn't automatically unfold. God is the author of divine purpose, but each of us plays a vital part in whether or not that purpose is realized.

Just as a newly conceived embryo needs the nurturing environment of its mother's womb to mature, divine dreams must also be nurtured in a healthy environment. That environment is your heart.

The Wellspring of Life

The Bible says "Above all else, guard your heart, for it is the wellspring of life."[1] Nowhere else in the Bible will you find the words *above all else*. Clearly, caring for our hearts should be a number one priority.

Although it's true that God has a purpose for your life, it's also true that that purpose doesn't automatically unfold. God is the author of divine purpose, but each of us plays a vital part in whether or not that purpose is realized.

Merriam-Webster defines *wellspring* as "a source of continual supply." Your heart is the fountain through which life's many streams flow. Whether this fountain emits sweet or bitter waters is entirely up to you, and—since those waters nurture your attitudes, beliefs, thoughts, and choices—ultimately, they mould your destiny.

Jesus said that when we receive him as Saviour and Lord, "streams of living water will flow from within."[2] Referring to the Holy Spirit who indwells believers, these streams of living water are rich with God's blessings, including purity, divine power, grace, love, wisdom, and faith. God designed the river of his Spirit to refresh, restore, transform, and empower every area of our lives—and to flow through us to bless others.

Many people, however, allow their hearts to become plugged by debris, hindering the flow of this river of life. Not realizing the importance of caring for their hearts, they allow the rubble of sin, worldliness, worries, bitterness, unbelief, and distractions to collect and block the flow of God's grace and power in and through their lives.

To reach our purpose, it's vital that we learn how to guard and nurture our hearts.

Heart Toxins

"You are what you eat" is not only a useful maxim for physical health, it also applies to spiritual health. If you regularly ingest "soul junk food," every area of your life will suffer. Considering that *all of life* flows from your heart, considering that your heart is the very seat of your dreams and the womb of your destiny—is it not worth investing time and effort to protect it from contaminants?

A caring expectant mother would never intentionally harm her unborn child by ingesting toxins or refusing a nutritious diet. Yet many people carelessly neglect their hearts, not realizing they are sabotaging their destiny. In the same way that physical toxins can damage an unborn child, "heart toxins" stunt the development of your gifts and potential.

In practical terms, how can we guard our hearts?

In biblical times, the word *guard* conveyed the imagery of a sentry defending a fortress. Alert and vigilant, sentries were responsible for keeping the city safe. If a sentry spied an enemy, he warned the appropriate authorities and employed weapons and other tactics to prevent enemies from penetrating the fortress.

Similar vigilance is required in guarding our hearts.

Heart toxins come in many forms. External sources may include books, television programs, and Internet sites promoting themes such as sexual perversion, hatred, rebellion, violence, and blasphemy.

A man struggling with sexual desire for his two young daughters went to a counsellor for help. During the counselling sessions, this man admitted to reading pornographic materials, including those depicting sexual acts between adults and children. He insisted there was no connection between his pornographic reading habits and the lust he felt toward his daughters.

"There's nothing wrong with reading pornography," he said. "It doesn't affect me. It can't hurt anyone." Though he suffered terrible guilt and confusion about his lust for his daughters, he refused to see how the junk he was feeding his mind was perverting his emotions.

Not surprisingly, studies have found that the majority of sex offenders are avid consumers of pornography.

The first and most important standard for determining whether something will be toxic to your heart is to answer this simple question: Does it contradict or undermine the values and truths taught in the Bible? (a no-brainer for such things as pornography, adultery, lying, cheating, and so forth).

For areas not specifically addressed in Scripture, God has given Christians the Holy Spirit, who dwells in our spirits. Jesus promised that the Holy Spirit will convict of sin and guide us into all truth.[3]

When you think about doing a certain thing, what happens in your spirit? Is there a sense of uneasiness or grieving, what some describe as "a check"? If so, run from it. A word of caution—if you habitually ignore these inner promptings, your spirit will become desensitized. The time may come when you no longer discern the warnings of the Holy Spirit, for repeated exposure to "soul junk food" hardens the conscience.

Internal heart toxins are just as deadly. These represent thoughts and emotions such as anger, bitterness, worry, hatred, pride, and impure lusts. If you succumb to these negative thoughts and emotions, your faith will weaken and you'll block the river of God's Spirit from flowing through your life.

The Bible admonishes,

Do not be deceived: God cannot be mocked. A man reaps what he sows. The one who sows to please his sinful nature, from that nature will reap destruction; the one who sows to please

50

the Spirit, from the Spirit will reap eternal life.[4]

Sow toxins in your heart, and you'll reap an endless litany of frustration and failure. But if you will sow the right spiritual nutrients, your heart will be nourished, your faith will grow, and your purpose will unfold.

Heart Nutrients

A responsible expectant mother is not merely concerned with avoiding

Internal heart toxins are just as deadly. These represent thoughts and emotions such as anger, bitterness, worry, hatred, pride, and impure lusts. If you succumb to these negative thoughts and emotions, your faith will weaken and you'll block the river of God's Spirit from flowing through your life.

alcohol and carcinogens, she is also conscientious about getting proper nutrition. She drinks more milk and eats more protein. She may take vitamins or other supplements. Often an expectant mother will also read articles or books about nutrition and exercise, investing time and effort in learning what she can do to ensure that her child will be healthy.

Likewise, it's vital that we invest time and effort in learning about the nutrients that will benefit our hearts. If we commit to a consistent diet of the right spiritual nutrients, our hearts will be nourished, our souls will be transformed, and our dreams will thrive.

Some people use the terms *soul* and *spirit* interchangeably, but they are different. The spirit is the part of us that receives the nature and eternal life of God when we are born again. In the New Testament, this new nature is described in many ways: the new creation, the new man, the new self, the law of the spirit of life in Christ Jesus in us, the inner person of the heart, and so forth. Your spirit is perfect, for the Holy Spirit in God's perfect image dwells there.

But even though our spirits are perfect, the Bible tells us that our souls (the mind, will, and emotions) must be renewed and transformed. Of course, this is a lifelong process that will not be completed until we see Jesus.

The Bible urges us to give ourselves continually to this work of renewal: "Be transformed by the renewing of your mind. Then you will be able to test and approve what God's will is—his good, pleasing and perfect will."[5]

Following are four powerful heart nutrients that will bring about inner transformation and ensure that the river of God's Spirit flows unhindered through your life. By no means is this an exhaustive list—that would require an entire book.

All of these "nutrients" have to do with cultivating a deeper friendship with God. God passionately desires intimacy with his children, and he has provided us with simple principles for developing that relationship. The greater the intimacy you cultivate with God, the more you will be filled with his Spirit. Your heart will be nurtured, and the river of life will flow unhindered, releasing your maximum potential.

Scripture Reading and Reflection

Imagine a tree planted by streams of what the Bible calls "living water," bearing fruit so abundant that the branches are bowed down by the weight. Its leaves never wither nor die, and no matter what the season or circumstance—whether there are droughts, floods, or snow—the tree never ceases to bear fruit.

The Bible uses this imagery to illustrate the fruitfulness we can experience as we regularly reflect on Scripture—the Bible calls this "meditation." The passage of Scripture goes on to say, "Whatever he does prospers."[6]

Throughout the Bible, "living water" symbolizes the fullness of the Holy Spirit. "Fruit" symbolizes spiritual and natural prosperity and effectiveness. Jesus said it is "to my Father's glory, that you bear much fruit." But he also preceded this with a condition that "you remain in me and my words remain in you."[7]

Regularly partake of the power-packed spiritual nutrients in the Word of God and you will grow spiritually and experience increasingly greater measures of success in every area of life.

You can do this through daily Scripture reading, study, and reflection. The Bible reminds us to "humbly accept the word planted in you, which can save you."[8] *The Message* paraphrase of this verse reads, "In simple humility, let our gardener, God, landscape you with the Word, making a salvation-garden of your life."

This Bible verse is not referring to our eternal salvation—that was guaranteed when we received Jesus Christ into our hearts. It refers to the transformation of our souls, an ongoing process by which our character, thoughts, beliefs, and attitudes grow more in harmony with the character of Christ.

I have personally found Scripture meditation to be a powerful tool for nurturing my heart and building my faith.

In some people's minds, the word *meditation* evokes the imagery of a monk chanting on a mountain or followers of transcendental meditation repeating mantras in their minds.

Scripture meditation is quite different. One meaning of biblical meditation is to "ponder" or "muse." In simple terms, this involves focused thinking, whereby we ponder, or reflect on, a verse or passage of Scripture in the Bible. We also consider how it to apply it to our lives.

Another biblical application of meditation is "to mutter." This has to do with repeating and praying Scriptures out loud. It includes singing praise songs based on Scripture.

I like to compare meditating to marinating meat. As the marinating liquids break down the fibres of the meat, the meat becomes tender and more easily absorbs seasonings. Meditating on Bible truths has a similar effect. It softens our hearts. It increases our capacity to absorb and understand truth. It sparks spiritual revelation, releasing life-changing power.

Jesus said, "The truth will set you free."[9] (He was referring to the Word of God—the Bible.) Freedom comes when truth penetrates the core of your identity and becomes revelation.

I discovered the power of Scripture meditation early in my Christian journey. At the time, I was struggling to understand and trust the unconditional love of God. I began taking time each day to meditate on Scriptures describing God's love and faithfulness. After several months, my insecurities about God's love were gone. Instead, I felt a deep and peaceful certainty of my worth in God's eyes. Truth had shone into the darkness of my heart, producing a life-changing revelation of God's amazing love for me.

Intellectual knowledge of the Bible is of little benefit. We need spiritual revelation of truth to experience its transforming power. Scripture says, "The word of God is living and active."[10] Scripture contains divine power that will penetrate the deepest places of the soul, dispelling darkness with truth and changing us from the inside out.

In addition to reflecting on Scripture during your private prayer time, you can meditate on Scripture anytime, anywhere. You don't have to be alone with God to do this. Think about Scripture verses throughout your busy day—while driving to work, standing in line at the bank, folding laundry, or doing repetitive tasks that don't require mental concentration. Meditation is like "daydreaming" about God and his Word.

Nourish your heart daily with the powerful Word of God. Meditate on it, ponder it, study it, speak it, and pray it. Listen to it on teaching tapes. Read good books that provide revelation about God's Word.

Your heart will thank you. Your dreams will thrive as you nourish them with the power-packed nutrition of God's Word.

Prayer

Prayer allows you to view life from the high vantage point of God's greatness, rather than focusing on impossible circumstances and personal limitations. Instead of looking up at your problems and feeling overwhelmed by their magnitude, you view them from the perspective of God's power and majesty.

The apostle Paul says,

> Do not be anxious about anything, but in everything, by prayer and petition, with thanksgiving, present your requests to God. And the peace of God, which transcends all understanding, will guard your hearts and your minds in Christ Jesus.[11]

As we focus on prayer and thanksgiving, God's peace fills our hearts and minds. The flow of his Spirit is unobstructed by anxiety, doubts, or fear. As our hearts remain at rest, we find it easier to trust in God and his promises.

Prayer is conversation with God. It doesn't get more complicated than that. While there are special ministries of intercession, when it comes to your own personal prayer life, you should think of prayer as conversation with God.

Conversing with God is not a science. It's a skill anyone can learn (as long as you have been spiritually born again through Jesus Christ). The more you practise, the better you get at it.

Start by setting aside some time each day for quiet communion with God. I prefer early mornings, before I become distracted by the busyness of my day, but some people prefer late at night or other times. Find what works for you.

How much time? Well, the more time, the better. A few rushed minutes here and there won't foster much intimacy with God, any more than it would cultivate intimacy with your spouse or child.

Like any conversation, prayer should involve both talking and listening. God encourages us to come to him with our petitions and needs, but he also wants us to listen and receive. What's the point of asking God for wisdom if we don't take time to listen?

God designed us to hear his voice and receive his grace. This is not something difficult or complex, nor is it reserved for "super-spiritual" people. It is a gift to every born-again child of God and should be as natural as breathing. The more time we spend quietly in God's presence, the easier it becomes to listen with our "spiritual ears" rather than with our intellect or emotions. Through practice, we train our spirits to discern God's leading. We learn to receive God's love and grace. We are empowered with supernatural strength to fulfill our callings.

The prophet Isaiah said, "Those who wait on the LORD Shall renew their strength; They shall mount up with wings like eagles, They shall run and not be weary, They shall walk and not faint."[12]

In our fast-paced, goal-driven society, many people find it hard to wait silently in God's presence. Feeling as though they must always be "doing something," the idea of taking time to simply wait on God makes them uncomfortable.

Waiting on God is not passive, however. It involves actively seeking God, drawing nearer to him, and treasuring time with him more than anything else. There's no better way to invest our time.

Jesus said that his followers know his voice.[13] He also promised that the Holy Spirit "will guide you into all truth . . . and he will tell you what is yet to come. He will bring glory to me by taking from what is mine and making it known to you."[14]

The problem is not that God doesn't speak to us; the problem is that many of us don't take the time to develop out "spiritual ears."

What does God's voice sound like? Well, it sounds a lot like Scripture, for God is the author of Scripture. As we read his Word, the Holy Spirit may enlighten us in a fresh way, imparting faith and courage, providing an answer to prayer for wisdom or direction, or convicting us of sin. The Bible calls this "revelation."

God's voice also sounds something like you, for it is your spirit being influenced by the Spirit of God. Sometimes God communicates with words, in what the Bible describes as "a gentle whisper." Another translation calls this "a still small voice."[15] This is not an audible voice but words that we understand and perceive in our spirits.

Another frequent way God communicates is through what many describe as the "inward witness" or "impressions," whereby we sense his direction and leading, but not in words. Jesus promised that the Holy Spirit would reveal things to us and guide us into all truth, but we must tune our spirit to listen and discern. Gloria Copeland wrote in *From Faith to Faith*, "Tune in today to that inward witness, to that quiet knowing, that urging, prompting, and leading arising within you." The more you practise, the easier it becomes to recognize God's leading.

Don't put God in a box, for he communicates in many different ways. For example, he may speak to you through nature. I'm not suggesting that nature itself speaks; rather, God may illuminate biblical truths through nature. For example, he may give you deeper revelation of the principle of spiritual sowing and reaping while you're weeding your garden. My friend Julene said she was inspired by watching the birds, as Jesus instructs us to do. It strengthened her faith to believe that God would provide for her needs.

Though it is important to have daily private devotional prayer, the Bible also says to "pray continually." How can we do that? Simply by cultivating the habit of conversing with God throughout the day, in every activity. Talk to him about everything. Thank him for his presence and love. Ask him for wisdom when you must make a decision. Enjoy developing the art of ongoing conversation with God.

Life is often like an out-of-tune radio blaring out irritating noise and static. We need to adjust the frequency so we can tune in to the presence of God that surrounds us. As we discipline ourselves to take breaks during the day to refocus on God's majesty, goodness, mercy, holiness, and amazing love, we train our spirits to be more sensitive to his leading and promptings.

As you spend time in God's presence each day, your heart will be nourished with divine power, grace, strength, and wisdom—providing fertile soil for your dreams to thrive.

Positive Thinking

A healthy heart is one that focuses on pure and positive thoughts. The Bible says, "For as he thinks in his heart, so is he."[16] In other words, your attitudes, beliefs, choices, actions, and destiny are a direct result of your thought life.

Focus on negative, critical, bitter thoughts, and you will become a critical, complaining, unthankful, depressed person. Focus on pure and positive thoughts and maintain a grateful attitude, and you will be a happy, positive person.

Next time you are feeling depressed, ask yourself, *What thoughts were going through my mind when I began feeling depressed?* Though other factors can cause depression, including hormonal fluctuations, chemical imbalances, and mental disease, depression is sometimes the result of dwelling on negative thoughts or emotions. Mind, emotions, and body are intricately interconnected. Negative thoughts will produce negative emotions; both negative thoughts and emotions can contribute to physical disease.

If you don't get control of your thought life, you'll find yourself defeated in many other areas of life.

"In military terms one could say the thought life is the command post," Dawn Jones wrote in her article "The Battle of the Mind." "This control center is the arena the enemy wants to infiltrate so he can defeat us in our thought-life, long before we are ever confronted in the fray."

Getting our thoughts under control can be challenging. The Bible tells us to "take captive every thought to make it obedient to

Christ."[17] Some people claim they have no control over the negative, depressing thoughts that play over and over in their minds. God would not tell us to take control of our thoughts if we lacked the ability to do so.

Some negative thought patterns are deeply ingrained and require aggressive confrontation. If you refuse to discipline your mind, over time, certain thought patterns will develop into what the Bible calls "strongholds." A stronghold is exactly what the term implies—deeply embedded destructive thought patterns that have a very *strong hold* on you. These are not easy to uproot. But the longer you wait to deal with them, the more difficult they will be to overcome.

Keep in mind that we have a spiritual enemy, Satan, who hates God and despises us—for we are the objects of God's love. Satan will attempt to dump on you thoughts of accusation, condemnation, deception, immorality, temptation, doubt, discouragement, and anger. These are all part of the enemy's arsenal.

You've likely heard the saying, "You can't stop a bird from pooping on your head, but you can stop it from building a nest there." Refuse to be intimidated by undesirable thoughts, for you can be sure that Satan will try and throw all kinds of ugly thoughts at you. You are not responsible for the negative thoughts that drop into your mind. You are, however, responsible for what you do with them. Don't dwell on them or act upon them.

The best way to deal with these thoughts is to get your mind on something else. The Bible provides practical advice on this.

Finally, brothers, whatever is true, whatever is noble, whatever is right, whatever is pure, whatever is lovely, whatever is admirable—if anything is excellent or praiseworthy—think about such things.[18]

Look for the good in people, for everyone has some positive qualities. Look for the good in your life and circumstances. Thank God continually for his blessing and love. Thank him for the wonderful promises in his Word—even if you are not yet experiencing the reality of those promises in your circumstances. Cultivating a grateful heart will go a long way toward training your mind to focus on pure, healthy, and life-giving thoughts.

When you bring your thoughts into harmony with the Word of God, his power and assistance are available to you. Character is developed as we make choices that resist sinful desires and temptations. The more we make these choices, drawing on God's power, the easier it becomes to get control of our thought life. As we discipline our minds to think positive, godly thoughts, we will also experience more emotional and physical health, and greater spiritual authority and effectiveness.

Some negative thought patterns are deeply ingrained and require aggressive confrontation. If you refuse to discipline your mind, over time, certain thought patterns will develop into what the Bible calls "strongholds." These are not easy to uproot. But the longer you wait to deal with them, the more difficult they will be to overcome.

Creative Activities

Finally, nurture your heart with creative activities and hobbies. Ask yourself, *What inspires me? What refreshes me? What stirs creativity and vision?*

For me, spending time in nature refuels my creativity and nourishes my heart. Besides reminding me of the awesome majesty of my Creator, nature calms my spirit and renews my faith.

If you love nature, schedule time on a regular basis to enjoy your favourite outdoor haunts. If you live in the city and find it difficult to get out to the country, find a park that you enjoy and make the time to visit there regularly.

If you love art, visit art museums. If you love music, attend concerts. If you love flowers, plant the biggest and most extravagant flower garden in the neighbourhood. Fill your home with flowers and give bouquets to friends and neighbours.

If you have always wanted to learn to paint, take a course. Who cares if you never sell a painting? That's not the point. The point is to find ways to cultivate and express the creative nature God placed in you.

When I was eleven years old, my grandmother gave me her piano. I loved taking lessons. My favourite pieces were romantic tunes like "Lara's Theme" from *Doctor Zhivago*, "Over the Rainbow," "Climb

Every Mountain." You get the picture—the more mushy, idealistic, pie-in-the-sky romantic, the better.

A few years after I became a Christian, I stopped playing the piano. I don't know why I stopped; I just did. Years passed. Then one day, during prayer, God spoke to my heart. *Why did you stop playing the piano?* I was surprised by the question. Immediately, a deep sadness filled me.

Since I'd never really thought about it, I had to search my heart for the answer.

When the answer came, it surprised me. I realized that I had stopped playing because I did not believe God was directing me to play the piano for ministry purposes or to help others in a meaningful way. Somehow, I had developed the legalistic attitude that it would be selfish for me to spend valuable time playing the piano purely for my own enjoyment.

I realized that playing the piano was one way of expressing the creativity God had placed in me. By repressing this, I was denying and rejecting a part of my God-created identity.

When I began to play the piano again (and I admit it—"Over the Rainbow" is still one of my favourites), my heart was nourished in fresh, new ways. I felt as though I was reconnecting with a core dimension of my identity.

Have you repressed creative pursuits because you felt they were a waste of time or irresponsible?

Remember, God's very essence is creativity. When you nurture your creativity, you are cultivating Christian character. You will also have more to give to others when you nurture your own heart.

Consider God's creativity in nature. Do you think he was concerned merely with the functionality of the ecosystem when he created thousands of varieties of wildflowers in every conceivable colour, pattern, and texture? God is utterly, undeniably extravagant. Creativity is God's essence; he can't help being extravagant with it. He *is* creativity. And so are you—for divine creativity is woven into the fabric of your soul. Find ways to cultivate and express it. Your heart will be nourished in the process.

Find at least one creative hobby and make it a part of your schedule. Never say that you don't have time. You'll be a better person, and you'll have more to give to your family and others if you take time to nurture your own heart.

Remember this: all of life flows from your heart. Your heart is the very seat of your dreams and the womb of divine destiny. God placed a river of life in you when you entered into relationship with Jesus Christ. By guarding and nurturing your heart, you will ensure that this live-giving river flows unhindered, enriching and empowering every area of your life.

For Personal Reflection or Group Discussion

1. Why do you think the Bible places such emphasis on guarding our hearts?

2. Most people understand the negative effects of external heart toxins, such as pornography or violent television programs, but many don't realize the destructiveness of internal heart toxins, such as negative thinking or bitter emotions. Can you think of a time when your thoughts or emotions caused depression or hindered your relationship with God? What advice would you give to someone who struggles with disciplining her thought life?

3. Give an example of how one specific "heart nutrient" discussed in this chapter has brought about positive change in your life.

4. What are some practical ways of applying Philippians 4:8 in daily life?

Chapter Five

The Restored Heart

*The true story of each person
is the journey of his or her heart.*

Brent Curtis and John Eldredge,
The Sacred Romance

T en-year-old Mary climbed out of her hard, lumpy bed shortly after midnight, shivering in the drafty room that reeked of stale alcohol. She crept down the hall to the bathroom shared by all the residents of the decrepit rooming house in downtown St. Catharines, Ontario. As the sticky floorboards creaked beneath her bare feet, Mary's heart began pounding like a sledgehammer. *What if mean old Mr. Runchen wakes up? Or that filthy man in room 210 who always tries to touch me?**

After using the bathroom, Mary raced back to the tiny two-room suite she shared with her parents and brother. Not that she felt safe around her parents—as usual, they were passed out in a drunken stupor. But at least it was better than being alone.

Crawling under the thin blankets that did little to keep out the cold, Mary tried to ignore the gnawing hunger in her stomach. As

---

* In Mary's story, the names of other individuals and some details have been fictionalized to protect privacy.

usual, the cupboards were empty. Sometimes she could find some bread or potatoes for a few days at the beginning of the month, but most of the time, any money her parents scrounged up was spent at the liquor store.

Anguished thoughts of shame and self-loathing tormented her as she tossed and turned, wishing, somehow, that she could make the pain go away. *What's wrong with me? What's so awful about me that Mom and Dad are drunk all the time? Why does Mom keep running away?* (Her mother would run away for months at a time.)

Mary began thinking about some of the other residents in the rooming house. *Why is Mr. Runchen so angry all the time? Did something bad happen to him?* Her thoughts turned to old Harry Morris. *He never says a word, just sits in a chair in the living room and stares out the window all day long. He never goes anywhere, and nobody ever comes to visit.* Molly, the waitress in 201, looked hard and worn out. *Why does she have to yell at her two little boys all the time? They always look so sad.*

Why is there so much pain in the world? Mary wondered. *Why does life have to hurt so much?*

Mary began to wonder if there was something she could do to help the residents of her rooming house. A dream began to form in her heart—a vision of a safe place where everyone would feel loved and protected, nobody would go hungry, and people could sleep in warm, safe beds. Night after night, she thought about her dream. She envisioned building a hospital that would meet everyone's needs on a piece of vacant land she had noticed in downtown St. Catharines.

There was only one problem—money. How would she pay for this hospital? *I know,* Mary thought, her little-girl's heart coming up with a perfectly logical solution. *I'll just collect a dime from every person in Canada. Everyone could afford that—even I have a dime once in while. Then I'll have all the money I need!*

For a time, Mary could dull the pain in her heart by thinking about her dream. Hope would flicker in her heart for those brief moments— hope for a better future for herself and for other hurting people.

But life kept getting worse. Years passed. All her time and effort was expended in the daily struggle to survive, her wounded heart hardly capable of focusing on anything else. Over time, Mary's dream faded.

Mary's feelings of inferiority and self-loathing worsened, amplified through sexual abuse and parental neglect. In her teen years, she dated boys who treated her like the trash she believed herself to be. "I didn't think I had value or worth. My choices reflected the low value I placed on myself."

When she was fourteen years old, Mary was seduced by a twenty-one-year-old man. Before long, he became controlling and abusive. "He would drive over a bridge and threaten to drive off into the water unless I promised to stay with him forever," Mary recalls. "Several times he brought out a gun and threatened to kill me if I ever left him. He ordered me to not see my friends."

The relationship continued until finally, at the age of eighteen, Mary thought, *I can't go on any more. I don't care if he kills me; I'm dead anyway.* She ran away in the middle of a cold winter night, not even taking time to put on shoes. Stumbling through the snow in her bare feet, she walked miles until she reached the home of a friend.

Several more abusive relationships followed until, at the age of twenty-three, Mary married. Unlike most of her previous boyfriends, her husband treated her with kindness and respect. "He was a very good and kind person. I longed for a home and family, but I was too broken to have a real relationship. I just wanted the pain to go away."

Though Mary bore two sons, the pain and emptiness worsened. Fear, her lifelong companion, dominated every waking moment and plagued her dreams at night. "I was afraid of everything—I was afraid of the dark, of being alone, of being with people, of even crossing the street. Fear was calling the shots in my life. My one and only concern was *Will I be safe?*"

In desperation, she began seeing a counsellor. "I thought I had finally found someone who could make it stop hurting. He told me that my whole problem was that I wasn't loved, that what I really needed was unconditional love." The counsellor encouraged her to cry; then he would hold her and comfort her.

After a few more sessions, the counsellor began telling Mary that he was the only one who could love her unconditionally. He convinced her that his love would heal her brokenness. Vulnerable, confused, and desperate for relief from the pain, Mary was easy prey, and the counsellor persuaded her to have an affair with him.

Before long, Mary's marriage split up, and her dream of an intact family was buried in the ashes of shame and despair.

Mary's life seemed like an endless cycle of self-destructive choices and tragedy. Her fragmented heart, vulnerable in its desperate cry for love and safety, made her an easy target for manipulation and abuse. Driven by emotional pain, she stumbled from one self-destructive choice to another. Consumed by the struggle to get through each day, Mary could never have believed that her life might have a purpose, that it was possible to live with joy, or that she could be free of the fear that plagued her day and night.

If that were the end of Mary's story, it would be terribly depressing. As you'll see later in this chapter, Mary's life took a dramatic turn.

The Wounded Heart

Nothing will hinder your ability to discern and embrace your destiny more than a wounded heart. It will sabotage your relationships, drive you to make self-destructive choices, and hinder you from discerning and fulfilling your purpose.

The cries of a wounded heart longing for affirmation drown out the gentle voice of God's loving purpose, propelling some people to pursue endeavours that clash with who they really are and paralyzing others with fear.

There's a world of difference between desires birthed by God and those spawned in a wounded heart. Inner brokenness begets a perpetual cycle of self-destructive choices, as was Mary's experience. Emotional wounds hinder us from distinguishing between holy, God-inspired passions and those that stem from emotional deficits.

Poisonous arrows strike us all, some more deeply and frequently. We are especially vulnerable during childhood, when the arrows of abuse, rejection, divorce, abandonment, tragedy, and lack of affirmation penetrate the very core of our identity. Once there, the arrows inject their toxins into our emotions and belief system.

Unhealed hurts fester, emitting lethal poisons that erode every area of life. These hurts form a point of reference for how we see ourselves, how we relate to others, and how we interpret all of life's choices and opportunities. What's more, they blind us to the holy desires and dreams God placed in our hearts.

It's a rare person who completes the journey to adulthood without picking up some arrows along the way. Even the best parents make mistakes, unintentionally wounding their children with criticism. Some parents, unaware of their children's desperate need for affirmation, unknowingly open the door of their children's hearts to the arrows of inferiority. Far more damaging are the wounds inflicted when parents or caregivers intentionally inflict emotional, physical, or sexual abuse.

If the arrows of life were not enough, we also have a spiritual enemy, Satan, who takes advantage of our wounds and uses them to accuse us, reinforcing messages of rejection, ugliness, pain, anger, and shame.

As Brent Curtis and John Eldredge wrote,

> As long as we do not admit that the deep things of our heart are there—the rejection and hurt, the shame and sorrow, the anger and rage—these rooms of our heart become darkened and the enemy sets up shop there to accuse us.[1]

Why does Satan hate us? We are God's beloved, the apple of his eye, and the reason Jesus died on the cross. Satan hates God. Naturally, he detests anything God values.

Jesus describes Satan as a thief who comes to "steal and kill and destroy."[2] Make no mistake. Satan is on a mission to steal your dignity, kill your dreams, and destroy your potential.

It would be terribly depressing if the message of Satan and the arrows were the end of the story. But it's not. The best chapter in this story proclaims the triumphant message of Jesus' finished work at the cross. As the apostle John says, "The reason the Son of God appeared was to destroy the devil's work."[3]

As you draw closer to Jesus, you develop a clearer revelation of the redemptive vision that he has for your life. Your faith grows, and you begin to really believe in his desire and ability to bring wholeness and purpose to every area of your life.

Psalm 23 tells us that the Lord restores our souls. Healing human brokenness is the heartbeat of our heavenly Father. That is why Jesus declared, "He has sent Me to heal the broken hearted, To proclaim liberty to the captives . . . . To set at liberty those who are oppressed."[4]

Jesus came to set imprisoned hopes free. Not only does he forgive our own sin, but he also sets us free from the inner hurts and dysfunction that result from the sins committed against us by others. He can heal every broken heart. He can unlock every chain of depression, bitterness, fear, inferiority, shame, and anger. He is the answer—the only answer—to breaking free from inner prisons. As your heart is restored, divine dreams grow and flourish.

Some people remain focused on their wounds, never moving on to apprehend the wholeness available to every child of God. Others believe and trust in Jesus' promise of healing and find complete restoration.

Mary's life is a beautiful portrait of the miracle of restoration. When I met her a few years ago, my impression was of a woman overflowing with joy and gratitude. In full-time ministry as a speaker, teacher, and counsellor, she was passionate about her mission to take the message of healing and hope to hurting people. When she wasn't talking about her greatest passion—her love for Jesus Christ—she was talking with joy and pride about her two sons, then teenagers.

I never would have guessed that Mary had suffered through such a dysfunctional childhood, for everything about her emanated faith and confidence.

Though Satan took advantage of the arrows that were lodged in her heart as a little girl, though for many years he convinced her she was a worthless, bad, fearful, shameful person, Mary came to know the power of Jesus Christ to set her free from the prison of her past.

It was a journey, of course. As she grew in her relationship with God, his truths penetrated her heart and dispelled the lies that had fractured her soul. As she learned to trust more deeply in her heavenly Father, his love healed the emotional deficits that were created in her childhood and amplified later through self-destructive choices. Over time, Mary's identity became more deeply rooted in the love of God, and she experienced increasingly greater measures of security, strength, and confidence.

Best of all, the guilt and shame are gone forever.

I've come out of my pain with a lot more compassion and strength—a depth I would never have had otherwise. Jesus has not only given me my life back, he has blessed me with the gift of ministering to others.

Over the years, as Mary experienced the ongoing miracle of restoration, she enjoyed discovering new qualities about herself that she never knew existed.

I thought I was a homebody, a fearful person. The first time I was asked to read a Scripture out loud in church, I was so terrified that I asked lots of people to pray for me. Now, I come alive when teaching. I am so grateful for God's faithfulness in uncovering the person he created me to be—the person hidden under the brokenness and fears.

One key to experiencing that freedom was her willingness to respond to God's leading, despite feelings of intimidation. For example, when she was first asked to join an overseas mission team, she was terrified; nevertheless she went, and she experienced wonderful new dimensions of freedom in the process.

I discovered that I'm an adventurous person, which amazes me. I also love pioneering new ventures. That's so opposite to the kind of person I thought I was. I thought I was the timid, cautious type who never wanted to try anything new, but God has shown me that I love adventure! I never knew that about myself, because I was so overcome by fears. As God has been healing me, and as I respond when he asks me to do something, he has drawn out all sorts of qualities, interests, and passions that I never knew I had.

Through all this, the Holy Spirit has unveiled divine dreams. Some she was unaware of, for they were buried under all the pain and fears. Others she had repressed, for she believed they were beyond her reach.

Now in her mid-forties, Mary lives every day with purpose and adventure. Impassioned about providing hope and vision to the broken and discouraged, Mary has a powerful anointing to help others break free of their past and embrace a purpose-filled future.

"I had always longed to be whole and to help others find restoration and healing. Not only has God healed me, but he has given me the privilege of helping others find wholeness."

Mary's story is a testimony of the restoration available to every child of God. The Bible makes it clear that God does not favour one individual over another. Our wounds do not have the final word, unless we allow them. Jesus has the final word. If you want to discern your true calling and purpose, be willing to admit areas of unhealed hurt. Yield your heart to Jesus, and trust him to heal and restore you. Regardless of what has happened in the past, he can create beauty and purpose in and through your life.

Heart restoration doesn't happen overnight. It starts with a decision to receive the gift of salvation that Jesus provided through his death on the cross. It grows through daily communion with our Lord as we nurture our hearts, as discussed in the previous chapter. It continues to mature as we obey God's Word and the leading of his Holy Spirit.

The Bible tells us to be transformed through the renewing of our minds.[5] In this verse of Scripture, "transformed" is translated from the Greek word *metamorphoo*—the root of the word *metamorphosis*.

I love the imagery in this word. During metamorphosis, radical inner changes occur in a caterpillar's cellular structure. Eventually, the tough, scaly skin breaks and cracks until it disintegrates. Out of the broken fragments of the crusty old skin emerges the butterfly, transformed from an ugly, crawling creature into one of exquisite, silken beauty. As the butterfly spreads its wings, it is liberated to experience new horizons of purpose and potential.

When we receive Jesus Christ as Lord and Saviour, the Holy Spirit begins a work of inner transformation. He cracks the hard, crusty skin of sin, negative attitudes, fear, bitterness, anger, and selfishness. New thought patterns and emotional foundations are formed. Then, like the butterfly, we are liberated to experience vast new dimensions of previously untapped divine potential.

As we cooperate with the Holy Spirit, he fills the dry and barren places of our hearts. We experience an inner revolution that radically alters our attitudes, relationships, and life choices. The flame of God's Holy Spirit ignites the seeds of divine dreams that were planted in our hearts before we were born. Over time, as we commit to nurturing our hearts and spending time in God's presence, those seeds blossom to maturity.

The wonderful by-product of a restored heart is the ability to discern God-inspired passions.

This does *not* mean that you should wait until your heart is completely whole before you seek to understand and pursue your purpose. Wholeness is a journey; so also is fulfilling your purpose. For this reason, I use the phrase *pathway of purpose* throughout this book. Purpose unfolds progressively as we grow in our relationship with God, as we are transformed from the inside out, and as we follow him one day at a time.

If you're waiting until you are completely whole to start using your gifts to help others, you may wait forever. Often, making the decision to start using your gifts is the very thing that exposes unresolved heart issues. This provides an opportunity to deal with any painful memories or unhealed wounds that have crippled you. As you step out in faith, God will affirm what he has already placed in you, and you will be propelled forward on your pathway of purpose.

Purified Passions

Heart restoration involves more than healing; it also means ongoing character development to handle the responsibilities that accompany the purpose God has for our lives.

In ancient times, silver was purified by prolonged exposure to intense heat. After heating silver to its liquid state, a silver refiner sat on a stool over the cauldron of liquid and stirred the mixture. As the fire burned hotter, impurities bubbled to the surface. From time to time, the refiner reached down with a flat ladle to skim off the impurities. As long as the image was muddy and rippled with flecks of slag, he knew he had to keep working.

71

The refiner knew his job was done when he could look into the cauldron and see a clear image of his own reflection in the shining silver.

The Bible uses the imagery of the ancient silver refiner to illustrate how God purifies our hearts. "For you, O God . . . refined us like silver."[6] Passions must be purified to achieve their divine purpose. Some people make the mistake of assuming that their desires will be instantly purified when they become Christians. Nothing could be further from the truth. True, the moment we are born again, we are forgiven of all our sin and unrighteousness. God's own righteousness is imputed to us.

Sanctification, however, has to do with holiness of thought, word, and deed. *Sanctified* means "wholly set apart to God." This is a lifelong process, not a one-time event. It occurs as we daily yield to the transforming work of the Holy Spirit and as we obey his Word and leading in everyday life.

As our character matures, our passions are purged of selfish motives. Our hearts are cleansed of pride and other contaminants. God is faithful to mould us into vessels with the spiritual resilience necessary to contain ever-increasing measures of his power and presence.

When God puts his finger on an area of sin or compromise in our lives, some people get discouraged and walk away from their dreams. However, unsanctified desires do *not* negate a calling; they merely reveal areas that must be addressed before that calling will reach its highest potential.

When I was twenty-seven years old, I felt as though I were living a dream. For several years, I had been working as a magazine journalist, first as a magazine staff feature writer and then as a freelance correspondent for several business magazines. During those years, God had blessed me with exceptional favour and success. I loved my work; it was a perfect fit for my talents and passions.

One morning during prayer, God spoke to my heart: "I want you to give up your journalism career." I was stunned! *That couldn't have been God speaking to me*, I thought. *God is the one who led me into this. He is the one who has opened so many doors and given me such success.*

Over the next few weeks, as I continued praying about this (hoping I had misunderstood God), I kept getting the same response: "Give it up. Trust me."

Oh, how I wrestled with this decision! *How can I give up my dream? Can I really trust God? Why would he ask me to do this? What good could possibly come of giving up my journalism career?*

Finally, however, I made the heart-wrenching decision to obey God. I prayed, "Lord, I don't understand this at all, but I want to honour you. I give it to you." Instantly, peace flooded my heart. Though my heart grieved over the loss of my dream, I was also certain of God's leading. I took steps to cancel my freelance contracts.

One week later, an editor of a top national magazine invited me to lunch. We met, and he offered me the opportunity to become a monthly correspondent for the magazine. Needless to say, I was flattered—writing for a magazine of this stature was a journalist's dream.

When God puts his finger on an area of sin or compromise in our lives, some people get discouraged and walk away from their dreams. However, unsanctified desires do not negate a calling; they merely reveal areas that must be addressed before that calling will reach its highest potential.

As I listened to him presenting his offer, thoughts swirled through my mind like a prairie blizzard. *Perhaps this is something like Abraham giving up Isaac,* I thought. *God was testing my heart. Since I proved my willingness to give up my dream, now he is giving it back to me.*

Still, these thoughts stirred intense discomfort in my spirit. As we ate our lunch, I quietly prayed in my heart. To my dismay, God made it very clear that I was to decline this offer.

As painful as it had been the previous week to give my dream to God, this was far more heart wrenching. My mind screamed that I was crazy to turn down such a great opportunity. But the peace in my spirit confirmed God's will.

Later, I prayed, *Now what, Lord? What do you want me to do now?* He directed me to start my own consulting company, handling public relations and corporate communications. There was minimal writing involved, nothing involving any creativity or challenge, and certainly nothing I enjoyed. It was the type of writing I could do with my eyes closed and my mind turned off.

Over the next few years, my desire to write diminished. Finally, it died altogether. I concluded that writing was not God's plan for my life. When he asked me to give it up, he must have meant forever.

What I didn't realize was that God was exposing my calling to the fires of sanctification. Like the ancient refiner of silver, he was stirring my passions over a fiery cauldron, skimming off impurities as they surfaced. During this time, God was teaching me to love him far more than my desires, dreams, hopes, and ambitions. He was also exposing and cleansing selfish motivations.

After a long time (about ten years—I guess I needed a lot more work than some people), God spoke to my heart during prayer that he was going to resurrect the dream to write—but it would be very different than before. It would be resurrected in the power of God, and I would depend on him, not on my natural talents.

You would have thought I'd be ecstatic by this revelation, but I wasn't. Frankly, I felt empty. The death to my dream was so complete that the desire to write had been extinguished long ago. I felt as though the dream I once cherished belonged to someone else— it seemed so remote and unreal.

Over the next few months, however, the desire to write was slowly rekindled. At first, it was a barely discernible flicker. Over time, it grew stronger and brighter until one day my heart once again burned with a passion to write.

However, this passion was altogether different from what I experienced before my lengthy sojourn in the fires of sanctification. Now my passion was truly set apart to Jesus and his purposes. Whereas in the past I depended primarily on my natural talents, I had learned to truly depend on God and yield my gifts for his purposes. Writing was no longer merely a means of expressing creativity or working in an occupation I enjoyed; it embraced the privilege of honouring God and serving him with my talents. I wouldn't trade this for all the success in the world.

I'm reminded of Jesus' words, "Unless a kernel of wheat falls to the ground and dies, it remains only a single seed. But if it dies, it produces many seeds."[7]

Dying to selfish ambition is painful, but the end result is glorious. Of course, this death is both a daily commitment and a lifelong process. The more we yield to it, the more we experience Jesus' resurrection power working through us.

You may be thinking, *Does God always ask us to give up our dreams?* I believe the answer to this question is both yes and no.

Yes, in the sense that he wants us to yield ownership of our dreams to him. But no, he does not always ask us to give up the actual dream. He works uniquely in each of our lives to achieve the goal of sanctification. The key is to remain humble and open to whatever he asks us to do.

Never fear the fires of sanctification. Will they hurt? You bet they will. Sometimes you will feel as though you are dying. After all, you *are* dying—to selfishness, pride, and other dark attitudes and thought patterns. Through it all, your heavenly Father is doing a deep and precious work, purifying your passions and preparing you to contain greater measures of spiritual authority and anointing than you could have previously handled.

Do you truly long for God to use you in powerful ways to influence others and expand his kingdom on earth? Do you truly want to make a difference in this world? Then yield to the Refiner, and allow him to remove anything that may block the fullness of his Spirit from working through your life.

The Tested Heart

The Bible says, "The LORD tests the heart."[8] Heart tests are one of the ways God matures our character to handle the privileges and responsibilities that accompany purpose-filled living.

Tests are never for God's benefit. After all, he's God. He already knows what is in our hearts. Tests are for our benefit, to reveal wrong, insincere, or divided motivations and attitudes. Squeeze a sponge and the gunk on the inside oozes to the surface. Heart tests work much the same way—pressures in the form of difficult circumstances squeeze hidden soul toxins to the surface where we can see them.

When things are going our way and everything we touch turns to gold, when everyone thinks we're wonderful, it is easy to think, *Wow, am I ever doing great. Have I ever matured spiritually. I've become such a kind and peaceful person. And wow, what a giant of faith I have become!* Of course, we don't think these words consciously; they reflect subtle attitudes of the heart.

The real question is, *What happens when we are buffeted by the winds of adversity, when nothing is going our way, and when people betray us?* Most of us are shocked by the ugliness that surfaces. I know I have been ashamed by nasty attitudes that surfaced during times of stress.

When those toxic attitudes are revealed, we can admit we have issues we need to deal with or we can make the far-too-common mistake of playing the blame game. Many people blame other people, stressful circumstances, or the devil for ornery behaviour, depression, impatience, anxiety, or anger.

Many years ago I was assigned to write an article about a new steel production company that supplied pipe to the energy industry. I learned about rigorous stress tests the company ran on each piece of pipe it manufactured. One procedure involved a "hydro test," in which water was pumped inside the pipe to a predetermined pressure. The pressure was maintained for a set duration of time; weaknesses or flaws in the pipe caused leaking or bursts of water.

Character flaws are also revealed through pressure. To repair these flaws, God must expose them; there's not much he can do if we are blinded to our weaknesses or if we have fallen into the habit of blaming others or circumstances.

I couldn't count the number of times I have responded poorly to pressure, but I have come to realize that my negative responses indicated character flaws I need to address.

How do you respond to pressure? Do you become irritable, impatient, angry, depressed, unkind, or frustrated? Instead of blaming others or your circumstances or satanic opposition, acknowledge the flaws and weaknesses that surface under pressure. Pray, *Lord, how do you want me to change? What do you want to do in me?*

After you deal with your heart issues, you will be in a position to receive God's wisdom about whether you should make practical changes in your circumstances, such as cutting back on a too-busy schedule, dealing with a relationship problem, or changing your eating habits to help balance your hormones.

Tests come in many forms. It is important that we recognize these tests so we can properly respond; otherwise, we may experience delays or even miss out altogether on some of the blessings God desires for us.

One of the most common tests—and the one that qualifies us most for being released into God's purposes—is the test of forgiveness. If you breathe, you will be betrayed. If you are alive, you will be hurt. Such is life.

There's more. If you long with all your heart to please God and truly make a difference for his glory—you'll be offended time and again.

It's easy to say we want to develop a more Christlike character, but, of all the qualities Jesus embraced, perhaps the most divine was expressed in forgiving those who mocked and crucified him.

Character flaws are also revealed through pressure. To repair these flaws, God must expose them; there's not much he can do if we are blinded to our weaknesses or if we have fallen into the habit of blaming others or circumstances.

Joseph is the classic biblical example of someone who learned how to respond to offence. As a teenager, Joseph received a vision that God was going to raise him to a position of great prominence. His brothers were jealous of his vision and sold Joseph into slavery. Then Joseph was falsely accused of adultery and thrown into prison, where he faced more trials and disappointments. In each situation, Joseph refused to give in to feelings of resentment or self-pity. He sought to honour God and serve others, regardless of how much injustice he suffered.

During this difficult season in his life, Joseph's character was refined, tested, and purified—preparing him to handle the tremendous responsibility and prosperity that God wanted to entrust to him many years later when he was elevated to the position of vice-regent of Egypt, second only to Pharaoh.

The depth of Joseph's character was demonstrated in his gracious response to his brothers when they came to Egypt seeking food because of a famine in their own land. Joseph extended love and forgiveness, assuring them that he harboured no bitterness.

Faith is another area where we will be tested time and again on the pathway of purpose. These tests may come in the form of difficult and painful circumstances, seemingly unanswered prayers, or lengthy delays in experiencing the fulfillment of God's promises. During these times, we can succumb to doubt and bitterness or we can learn to trust on a deeper level than ever before.

Closely linked to the test of faith is the test of patience. Faith and patience go hand in hand, as you likely have discovered. As the Bible says, we must "imitate those who through faith and patience inherit what has been promised."[9]

Be careful that you do not get impatient and try to make things happen on your own. Many people, when going through difficult times, try to run from the pain by getting a new job, finding a new spouse, moving to a new city, or finding a different church. Rather than dealing with heart issues, they try to dull the pain and unsettledness by changing their circumstances.

Another common test is criticism or lack of affirmation from those you love or respect. Perhaps when you shared your dreams for the future, people responded with critical, undermining comments or even worse—indifference. You felt crushed, discouraged, hurt, and rejected. You can fail this test by giving up and becoming bitter. Or you can pass it by letting go of bitterness and purposing in your heart to pursue your calling.

Your integrity will be tested. It is easy to obey God when things are going well. When you've lost your job, or your business has gone under and the bills are piling up, what do you do? Do you stop giving to God's work? Do you cheat on your income tax? Do you compromise your values?

Continue to trust God in times of adversity. Be careful to avoid hardening your heart. Guard against a critical, complaining spirit, and trust him to complete the work he has started in you.

One of my favourite proverbs says, "Trust in the LORD with all your heart and lean not on your own understanding; in all your ways acknowledge him, and he will make your paths straight."[10]

The Valued Heart

Your heart is infinitely precious to God, more valuable than all the wealth in the universe. He is passionately committed to restoring, healing, and purifying your heart so that he can bring to pass all the wonderful purposes he has planned for your life.

The apostle Paul reminds us that "We are God's workman-ship."[11] The Greek word from which *workmanship* was translated means "a grand, epic poem."

Consider yourself an ongoing work of art. I love the way Corrie Ten Boom compared the transforming work of the Holy Spirit to a tapestry. If you look at the back of a tapestry, you see formless knots, rips, and clumps of thread. There's no pattern or beauty. But when you turn the tapestry over, you see a beautiful pattern of colour and harmony.

God has the power—if we let him—to take the good, bad, and ugly parts of our lives and weave them together into a beautiful tapestry of purpose. If your heart has been wounded, place it in God's healing hands. You can truly trust in his infinite love for you— a love that will never violate, reject, humiliate, or hurt you. With the utmost gentleness, he will tenderly invade the recesses of your heart with his healing oil, filling the caves of pain and shame with his lib-erating, restoring light.

When God exposes dark areas of selfishness and sin, don't suc-cumb to self-condemnation. It is because of his great love for us that God shines his light into the dark and fragmented areas of our hearts, so that we can be set free to experience the glorious liberty of children of God. This is the freedom that comes when our hearts are truly set apart to his purposes.

As your heart is healed, restored, and sanctified, you will be pro-pelled further along on the wonderful pathway of purpose that God has marked for your life. Trust him, for he will never fail you.

For Personal Reflection or Group Discussion

1. What impact did Mary's story have on you?

2. In your spiritual journey, has God revealed areas of brokenness that he desires to heal? Can you see ways that God has been restoring those areas?

3. Most of us desire to develop a more mature and holy character. What is one specific way that God has worked in you like the

ancient silver refiner, exposing areas of sin or compromise that you needed to deal with?

4. All of us are offended or betrayed from time to time. How has forgiveness, or unforgiveness, affected your life?

Chapter Six

Embracing Change

When you're finished changing,
you're finished.

Benjamin Franklin

One night, I dreamed I was cleaning my basement to prepare for a move to a new home. In my dream, which seemed to go on all night, I sorted through stacks of boxes, junk, knickknacks, and endless reams of paper.

I sensed an urgency to get rid of the clutter. Though most of it had served a useful purpose at one time, now it was just taking up space. I discarded unmatched dishes from my college years, old appliances that no longer worked, hardened nail polish and half-used lipsticks, knickknacks I had never liked but kept because they were gifts, film-developing solutions left over from when I set up my own darkroom, several boxes of legal and financial papers from a business I once ran, and other miscellaneous papers and junk. Every so often the tedium was interrupted by the discovery of a long-forgotten treasure such as an old diary or photo album.

On and on my dream went. At long last, I finished my task. What a wonderful sense of accomplishment I felt! Shaking the grime and dust off my clothes, I left the basement.

Suddenly, my dream switched to a new scene. I stood on the threshold of a bright, spacious new home, featuring all my favourite colours and decor. Fresh flower arrangements filled the foyer. As I walked inside, a soothing sense of freshness swept over me like a warm spring breeze.

I woke from my dream, and immediately I sensed these words in my heart: "Out with the old; in with the new."

As I pondered this dream and prayed about its significance, I felt prompted to read the story of two Bible prophets, Elisha and Elijah.[1] Elisha longed to experience the supernatural power he saw evidenced in Elijah's ministry. When he expressed his desire, Elijah responded, "You have asked a difficult thing."

It's not that Elijah didn't want Elisha to experience the power of the Holy Spirit that characterized his own ministry—after all, he loved Elisha like a son and had been grooming him to take over his ministry. He also wanted him to seriously consider the responsibility that went along with it. Greater measures of God's power always require deeper levels of commitment and consecration.

Having witnessed the life-changing results of Elijah's ministry, Elisha was ready to pay the price.

Later, as they walked together, Elijah was taken up to heaven in a whirlwind. In response, Elisha immediately removed his own clothes and tore them to pieces. I was intrigued by the finality of this act—by ripping up his clothes, Elisha could never wear them again.

Next, he donned the cloak that had fallen from Elijah. Immediately, Elisha received a fresh touch of the Holy Spirit's power, evidenced when he struck the waters of the Jordan with the cloak, crying, "Where now is the LORD, the God of Elijah?" The waters parted, and Elisha crossed over to the other side.

As I prayed about how this passage of Scripture applied to me, I sensed that Elisha's old clothes represented stagnant areas of my life I needed to discard. The cloak represented a new spiritual season that God was leading me into.

Some of the stagnant areas once served a worthy purpose, but, having completed their purpose, they had become stale. Like dead foliage in autumn, they were cluttering my heart and blocking new growth. Some reflected negative mindsets, such as doubt and unbelief. Some represented memories of failure I dredged up from time to time. Others represented aspects of my work and ministry that no longer bore fruit.

I stood at the threshold of a new spiritual season. To fully experience the new things God desired for me, I had to turn away—once and for all—from previous seasons.

Spiritual seasons are much like natural seasons in that they are constantly changing. Change, as I'm sure you have discovered, is a prerequisite to growth.

I was reflecting on this principle last autumn while walking along my favourite path through a grove of aspen. I felt despondent as I listened to shrivelled leaves crackling under my feet. Each harsh, crunching step warned of impending cold and snow—another long, barren, Canadian winter.

I picked up three leaves and unfurled them. Crafted on each was an image of its mother tree. A thick trunk stem stretched vertically, supporting an intricate web of main branches and sub-branches. The sun penetrated the thin, transparent skins and illuminated surprising nuances of brown, rust, plum, and gold.

One dark, plum-brown leaf, elongated and narrow, felt dry and scratchy. Rounded and golden, the second leaf was edged by a lacy half-circle pattern. The third leaf was asymmetrical and bent to the left, as though weary from life's burdens.

Joy replaced my sadness as I realized that each shrivelled leaf reflected life's changing seasons. Each carried images of the sweet promise of spring, the strength and confidence of summer, the mellow joy of autumn, and the barrenness of winter. Though winter is indeed harsh and cold (at least in most parts of Canada), it is also the time when the dead leaves are absorbed into the frozen soil, decaying and breaking down into minerals and other nutrients necessary to nourish new life in spring.

As Scripture reminds us, "There is a time for everything, and a season for every activity under heaven."[2]

Shed the Old

I love the beauty and fragrance of cut flowers. In summer, our house looks like a garden centre, with vases of cut flowers displayed on the coffee tables, dining table, our bedroom dressers, and any other flat surface I can find. I love flowers so much that I try to squeeze every last morsel of life out of them, reluctant to throw them out until they actually begin to stink.

What about you? Do you tend to hold on to things long after they have served their purpose? If so, you are not alone. It is human nature to resist change. Flexibility is something we must learn.

But if you refuse to let go of the past, the very things that once emitted beauty and fragrance will begin to rot. Worse, they will hinder you from experiencing the new things that God wants to do in and through you.

There is a passage of Scripture that I love:

Forget the former things; do not dwell on the past.
See, I am doing a new thing!
Now it springs up; do you not perceive it?[3]

This passage contains not only a promise but also a warning: "Do you not perceive it?" If we remain stuck in the past, we will never recognize—much less embrace—the new things that God wants to do in our lives.

Recently, I went for a professional facial, a birthday gift from my sisters. The cosmetician, Gerta, was obviously passionate about her art, for she explained in detail the chemical components of each product and how they worked on my skin.

One of those products was an exfoliating agent. Gerta lectured me about my hit-and-miss skin care program, warning that I should be exfoliating my skin at least once a week. "Exfoliation removes the outer surface of dead skin cells," she said. "If this isn't done on a regular basis, the dead skin cells clog up the pores, hindering circulation and preventing new skin cells from forming." Dead skin cells can also cause infection and blemishes, she added.

After exfoliating my skin and applying a toner, Gerta gently massaged my skin with a rich, soothing moisturizer. "Exfoliation prepares the skin to absorb moisturizing creams more deeply," she said. "It nourishes the skin cells, fostering new growth."

Later that evening, as I revelled in my soft, glowing skin, I realized there were fascinating parallels between dead skin cells and stagnant issues of the heart.

Live skin cells perform an important function, but once they have served their purpose and die, they become clogging agents that prevent new growth. In other words, the very cells that once pulsed with life become the agents of death.

Similarly, our hearts can be clogged with the dead foliage of things that were once vibrant and integral to God's purposes for us. But after serving their purpose, they become rotting compost that clogs our hearts and prevents new growth.

I made up my mind that I would give myself a regular "heart exfoliation." Periodically, I pray and ask God to reveal stagnant areas of my heart and life that I need to discard. I regularly ask myself these questions: *Am I living in the past? Am I holding on to negative memories? Am I clinging to something that has become stagnant?*

For several years, my friend, whom I will call Janet, talked incessantly about the "good old days" when her children were young and she was a full-time mother and homemaker. With her grown children having left the nest to start their own families, Janet moped around her house each day, unhappy, bored, and depressed. Devoid of any vision or sense of purpose, she developed a critical, complaining spirit.

Janet's obsession with the past immobilized her. Then one sleepless night, God showed her how she was wasting her time and talents. He impressed on her heart that it was time to let go of the past and move on. The season of motherhood was over; she could never go back. She needed to let it go. Over the next few months, Janet experienced a resurgence of joy, a renewal of vision, and the motivation to use her gifts and explore new challenges.

Paul the Apostle wrote toward the end of his life, "But one thing I do: Forgetting what is behind and straining toward what is ahead, I press on toward the goal to win the prize for which God has called me heavenward in Christ Jesus."[4]

Notice the energy implied in the words *straining* and *press on*. Truly, effort is involved in turning away from the past and pressing forward to achieve one's call.

Letting go of the past also means laying aside past successes. Don't build an altar to your accomplishments. Be willing to admit when something that once blossomed with life has become stale. It may be a job, a ministry, or another vocation. Has it stopped bearing fruit? Let it go.

It also means releasing—once and for all—painful memories, bitterness, and anger. It means turning away from proud and self-glorying thoughts and attitudes.

Some of the most difficult things to let go of are self-reproach and regret. We tend to be our own worst enemies. Though in our heads we know God has forgiven us of past sins and bad choices, in our hearts we struggle to forgive ourselves. We punish ourselves with guilt and self-condemnation, not realizing this mocks the price Jesus paid to forgive our sins.

Nail those memories in a coffin. Lay aside the guilt and self-condemnation. Bring those past hurts to the cross, give them to Jesus, and leave them there.

Make room for your future by letting go of your past. Ask God to release the fire of his Holy Spirit to sweep through your life and burn all the rotting weeds that clutter your heart. Then get ready to be launched into a new season of growth and blessing.

Step Out of Your Comfort Zone

Researchers at the University of California at Berkeley did an experiment some time ago that involved introducing an amoeba into a perfectly stress-free environment: ideal temperature, optimal concentration of moisture, and constant food supply. The amoeba lived in an environment that required no adjustment whatsoever. Yet, oddly enough, the amoeba died. Apparently there is something about all living creatures that demands challenge.[5]

Reaching our purpose requires stepping out of our comfort zones. It means accepting God's timetable, which, as you may have discovered, is rarely the same as ours.

I have had to learn this lesson time and again. Though I was adventurous to the extreme in my teens and early twenties, having embarked on many adventures—including backpacking alone through Europe—somewhere along the way I became resistant to change. I developed the attitude that change is acceptable if—and only if—I have all the time I think I need to prepare and adjust.

My tendency to drag my feet was evidenced a number of years ago when my husband and I were leading a Bible college. When we first accepted the position of dean, the college was tiny, with only about thirty students. But within three months of taking the position, enrollment had increased fivefold. We also implemented a new degree program in conjunction with an accredited university, which meant we had to rewrite most of the courses to meet the accreditation requirements.

Though we had excellent instructors, our initial budget had no room for hiring additional administrative support. Besides overseeing the college and students, teaching, writing curriculum, counselling, and implementing new programs, we also handled most of the administration. Needless to say, it was challenging and strenuous work.

Some of the most difficult things to let go of are self-reproach and regret. We tend to be our own worst enemies. Though in our heads we know God has forgiven us of past sins and bad choices, in our hearts we struggle to forgive ourselves. We punish ourselves with guilt and self-condemnation, not realizing this mocks the price Jesus paid to forgive our sins.

After a few years of really slugging it out, things were finally running smoothly and we had all the staffing support we needed. This freed us to focus on planning, teaching, and counselling. I remember thinking how easy it had become. (Perhaps that was my first mistake.) I also remember thinking how lovely it was to enjoy this season of clear sailing in calm waters.

About six months later, my husband and I began to sense that God was preparing us for another major change. I tried to push those thoughts aside, not wanting anything to rock my now-comfortable little boat. *We've been through enough changes*, I thought. *It's time to relax.*

Another few months passed. Then one September morning in my prayer time, God spoke to my heart, "Judy, change is coming sooner than you think."

Oh, please Lord, not too soon, I prayed. *I can't handle any big changes right now.*

Later that same day, my husband, Brian, said, "Honey, I sense

God wants us to give up the college at the end of the fall semester. I believe God is directing me to start a new ministry in the political arena in Canada. And I believe the first step is to release the college at the end of the semester."

For several years, it had become increasingly evident that Brian had a political calling, so that was no surprise. But the end of the fall semester? That was only three months away! (When God said "soon," he wasn't kidding.)

My stomach knotted with anxiety. Though my spirit witnessed with Brian's words, as God had already been nudging me about change, my mind and emotions were in turmoil. I felt as though my world was about to be shaken by a major earthquake. Anxious thoughts swirled through my mind: *What would we live on? How is this going to work out?* To me, it was happening much too quickly.

Just one hour later, we received a telephone call asking us if we would pick up my brother, Ken, and his travelling companion, Jim, at the airport as they arrived home from a mission trip to Russia.

Brian and I had not met Jim, who is recognized by many church and ministry leaders as a prophet. We picked them up at the airport and took them back to Ken's house. As soon as we walked in the door, Jim began to speak to us. We had not told anyone, including my brother, that we were sensing change.

Jim said, "Brian, I see God raising you up as a voice in this nation. Change is coming—I see God closing one door and opening another in December or January." He went on to say many other things that specifically confirmed the direction Brian had been sensing.

Then he turned to me and said, "Judy, your stomach is knotted with anxiety. You know God has spoken to you about change, but you're afraid of the unknown. Trust God. Let it go. God is closing one chapter and opening another, but you need to trust him in this." He also talked of new things God was going to birth through my life that confirmed secret dreams of my heart that I had not shared with anyone except my husband.

Though I had been stubbornly dragging my feet, fearing the unknown, Jim's words were like a sword piercing through my excuses and confirming what I already knew in my spirit. Over the previous few months, God had been gently prodding me to be more flexible, but I had allowed my fears to hold me back.

Embracing this new season meant stepping out of my comfort zone. My husband had no problem taking the plunge; he has always been the courageous type who responds immediately to whatever direction God gives him. But for me, the idea of leaving a secure, salaried position to step into the unknown provoked considerable anxiety.

The subsequent years proved to be the most challenging and frightening—yet the most amazing, wonderful, and faith-building—of our entire Christian walk. As we stepped out to pioneer this new venture, we experienced the miracle-working power of God time and again.

People often say we should live by faith. It's one thing to say it; it is another to actually live it. When you launch something new that God has impressed on your heart, you discover for yourself the exciting adventure of walking by faith.

Living by faith means being willing to move when God says "Move." Over the years God has brought me to a place where I actually anticipate change. He has also brought me to a place where I don't need to have all my ducks in a row. I am finally applying the advice of a dear pastor friend, who once said to me, "Judy, blessed are the flexible, for they shall never break."

These changes did not happen overnight—God has worked in me through many circumstances over the years to cultivate the willingness and desire to step out of my comfort zone.

Embrace the New

You may have heard the story of two caterpillars that were crawling across the grass when a butterfly flew over them. They looked up; one nudged the other and said, "You couldn't get me up in one of those things for a million dollars."

Like the caterpillar, fear of the unknown can blind us to our destiny. To experience the benefits of spiritual transformation, we must passionately desire change. We must be willing to try new things.

"If you play it safe in life, you've decided that you don't want to grow," said American lawyer and judge Shirley Hufstedler.

If you truly want God to release you into your divine purpose, you can be sure that he will direct you to do things that threaten your sense of security. Why? He wants you to learn to truly depend on him—not your bank account, talents, intelligence, relationships, or good looks.

Self-reliance is the opposite of God-dependence. Self-reliant people dislike the feeling of being out of control and tend to resist the inner promptings of the Holy Spirit to step out in faith. This hinders the power of God from flowing freely through their lives.

Humility is reflected in trusting and depending on God, regardless of how insecure or out of control this may cause you to feel. If God has revealed something new that he wants you to do, do it now. Don't wait until you have all your ducks in a row.

Be willing to try new things. Treasure change over safety. The desire for security will stand between you and noble achievements. As Kathleen Norris wrote in the January 2004 issue of *O Magazine*, "Disconnecting from change does not recapture the past. It loses the future."

Our friend Gail worked for a number of years as a telephone customer service representative. Her workday consisted primarily of sitting in her little cubicle, dealing with customer requests and complaints, and filling out paperwork. Though others with a different personality might have enjoyed this environment, Gail was bored and frustrated. She dreaded going to work each day. An extrovert, she loves to be around people and thrives in social situations. Despite having received promotions and raises, Gail resigned from her job and accepted a much-lower-paying position as a social worker.

Financially she is not richer, but she is wealthy in all the ways that truly matter. She loves getting up in the morning to go to work. Her new job has stirred untapped reservoirs of creativity and vision. Gail would never have tapped into these fresh fountains of purpose if she were not willing to step out of her comfort zone.

Another friend, Karen, ran her own business for a number of years, coordinating major events for non-profit organizations. She enjoyed her work; her business prospered; and she had many opportunities to share her faith.

The time came, however, when Karen sensed change. Although her business was doing well, she sensed God leading her in another direction. When she was approached to apply for a part-time position with an international children's ministry, she felt compelled to do so. After several months of working there, she reluctantly admitted to herself that when it came to her business, she was now bored; the vision and motivation to run her business was gone.

In a little over a year, she shut down her company and accepted a full-time position in marketing and public relations with this ministry. Having found her life calling, she is experiencing joy and fulfillment that she never dreamed possible.

Does that mean Karen was out of God's will during the years she ran her business? Of course not—launching and running a business was exactly in line with God's purpose for her during that season of life. She acquired valuable skills that prepared her for the next season.

Be willing to try new things. Treasure change over safety. The desire for security will stand between you and noble achievements. As Kathleen Norris wrote in the January 2004 issue of O Magazine, "Disconnecting from change does not recapture the past. It loses the future."

God has directed my husband and me through several major transitions, each requiring faith, risk, and obedience. Each new season has produced deeper reliance on God and a greater release of his anointing through our lives. God never forced those changes on us. He revealed the path before us and left it up to us to choose whether we would remain stuck in a rut of security and comfort or walk farther along the pathway of purpose.

That's a bit sobering, when you think about it. God leaves it up to us to choose whether to accept or reject our destiny. There is a price, and not everyone is willing to pay it. That is tragic—for the pathway of purpose is full of adventures in faith that I wouldn't trade for anything.

To embrace the new mantle of authority and purpose God has for us, we must also increase our expectation of the miraculous. God isn't impressed by what human ability alone can accomplish; he longs to reveal the greatness of his power and glory.

91

When you read Jesus' words that his followers will do great works, believe them.[6] Begin to expect this in your own life. When you read the Bible's promise that God wants to do "immeasurably more than all we could ask or imagine, according to his power that is at work within us,"[7] believe it. Expect it.

Don't focus on your personal limitations or circumstances. When Sarah heard God's promise to Abraham that she would bear a child, her first response was to laugh. How absurd! She was a very old woman who had always been barren. But God said, "Is anything too hard for the LORD?"[8] Sarah had to switch her focus from her personal limitations to the greatness of God.

God doesn't pick favourites. He calls you his own special treasure, and he wants to do amazing things through you. Never say you are unworthy, for he made you worthy through his sacrifice on the cross.

Increase your expectations. As they grow, you will find it easier to discern and respond to divine opportunities.

Allow change to position you for greater adventures in God. Change always precedes growth, and each level of growth expands your ability to handle greater measures of God's power and effectiveness. Rather than fearing change, anticipate it. Embrace it. Flow with it. Expect an adventure with God, today, tomorrow, and every day for the rest of your life.

For Personal Reflection or Group Discussion

1. Is there an area of your life that has become stagnant? How is it affecting you?

2. Is there anything from your past that is keeping you from experiencing new things God may have for you?

3. Do you fear change? Why?

4. Is God prompting you to step out of your comfort zone? What is one step you will take to respond?

Chapter Seven

Unfolding Vision

Dreaming illustrates your hidden capacities and unawakened ability.

Peter Daniels

L ate one night, I was walking on a wooded mountain path near my parents' home in the Rocky Mountains. A full moon glimmered through the partly overcast sky, casting a soft, muted beam on the path before me as far as the next bend, about a hundred feet ahead. Its soft rays also revealed a shadowy outline of the surrounding woods. My flashlight provided much brighter illumination of the path directly before me, helping me avoid stumbling over a rock or snagging my foot in a gopher hole. When I reached the next bend, the path wound sharply to the right. Once I passed the corner, the moon lit up the next leg of the path, which veered up a sharp incline.

As I enjoyed my stroll through the dark woods, I was reminded of the Bible verse: "Your word is a lamp to my feet and a light for my path."[1]

Like my flashlight, God guides my next steps, keeping me from stumbling or veering off in the wrong direction. Like the soft moon rays, he also provides general illumination of my broader purpose—

enough direction to complete the present leg on my journey. Once I reach the next bend and it's time to change direction, he will show me all I need to know then.

Progressive Revelation

God unfolds vision in many ways. One way of looking at it is like the pieces of a puzzle. To see the whole picture, you must fit each piece into its place. One of those pieces reflects your passions and gifts (which we will discuss in the next chapter). Another piece of the puzzle reflects your spiritual maturity and character development.

A central piece of this puzzle is divine revelation. After all, we are limited in understanding ourselves. Divinely inspired passions may be repressed by "the message of the boxes." They may be motivated by unmet emotional needs, or they may be cloaked by spiritual immaturity.

God, who created you, knows you far better than you could ever know yourself. You can never truly know yourself—or your passions, gifts, and calling—without also intimately knowing God.

Revelation lifts passion to a much higher level. It illuminates God's purpose for those passions.

In the Bible, Paul the Apostle prayed that believers would receive the "spirit of wisdom and revelation." Why? First, to know God more intimately, and second, to understand the calling and spiritual treasures he has placed in us.[2] *The Message* paraphrase of these Bible verses says "to make you intelligent and discerning in knowing him personally, your eyes focused and clear, so you can see exactly what it is he is calling you to do."

According to *Strong's Exhaustive Concordance of the Bible*, in this passage of Scripture, *revelation* is translated from the Greek word *apokaluyi*, which means laying bare, making naked, and disclosing truth about things before unknown.

God is not trying to hide your gifts or calling from you. He *wants* you to understand your purpose, but this revelation is discerned spiritually, not mentally. It generally unfolds over time, becoming more clear, focused, and detailed in stages—as you continue in prayer, as you are faithful and obedient to everything God asks you to do, and as you mature spiritually.

I strongly urge you to keep a journal. In my journal, I write down anything I sense God revealing to me or speaking to my heart. When I read my journal entries back through the years, a clear pattern emerges. My faith is encouraged as I see how God has faithfully provided more focused vision of my purpose over time.

Rarely does God provide us with clear and detailed vision of our distant future. For one thing, we couldn't handle it. For another, he wants us to trust him and depend on him each step of the way. We need to cultivate obedience, trust, maturity, and faithfulness to handle the responsibility that accompanies greater measures of God's power and anointing. Typically, God reveals purpose progressively as we are faithful to steward the vision he has already given us, as our character matures, and as we grow in faith.

Many people, not understanding the principle of progressive revelation, give up on their dreams. Some get frustrated when they can't see the whole picture. Others succumb to discouragement when they face obstacles and delays.

Most biblical faith heroes discerned their calling progressively over time. Vision of their purpose—including specific details—unfolded and expanded over many years as they obeyed God each step along the way.

Take Abram, for instance (whose name God later changed to Abraham).[3] The first instruction God gave Abram was to leave his homeland, and go "to the land I will show you." God didn't provide Abram with details about what the land would be like or what he would do once he got there. At first, all Abram received was one instruction and a general promise that God would make Abram's name great and bless all the nations of the earth through him.

Over many years, God provided more details about Abram's calling.

Abram sometimes struggled to believe the promise God had given him. Several years after Abram left his home-

> *Rarely does God provide us with clear and detailed vision of our distant future. For one thing, we couldn't handle it. For another, he wants us to trust him and depend on him each step of the way. We need to cultivate obedience, trust, maturity, and faithfulness to handle the responsibility that accompanies greater measures of God's power and anointing.*

95

land, God appeared to him again to remind him of the promise. Abram responded the same way many of us respond when we are feeling discouraged by delays or personal limitations: instead of believing in faith, he focused on his bleak circumstances. "O Sovereign Lord," he said, "what can you give me since I remain childless? . . . so a servant in my household will be my heir."

God replied, "This man will not be your heir, but a son coming from your own body will be your heir."

At this point, Abram was very old, and his wife Sarai was not only elderly, she had always been barren. You can imagine how pie-in-the-sky God's promise must have seemed. Humanly speaking, it was impossible.

God encouraged Abram's faith by taking him outside and saying, "Look up at the heavens and count the stars—if indeed you can count them." Then God said, "So shall your offspring be."

I wonder how Abram felt as he gazed at those stars. Did he feel overwhelmed by their number? Was he reminded of the greatness, glory, and majesty of his Creator? We know Abram was stirred to deeper levels of faith and vision, for the next verse says, "Abram believed the LORD, and he credited it to him as righteousness."[4]

That's not to say Abram's faith never again wavered. It was another sixteen years before he received the promise, and during that season of waiting Abram sometimes succumbed to doubt. At times, he tried to make things happen on his own. But through successes and failures, through times of believing and times of doubt, Abram's faith and character continued to mature, preparing him to handle the blessings and responsibilities that accompanied his ultimate calling.

God never gave up on Abram, nor does he ever give up on us. He is not looking for perfection; he's looking for humility and commitment, reflected in the willingness to change and grow.

Faithfulness

God will not give you additional vision and responsibility if you are not faithful with what you already have. Many people have big dreams but short-circuit those dreams through unfaithfulness.

Scripture warns us, "Now it is required that those who have been given a trust must prove faithful."[5]

Faithfulness has to do with reliability, diligence, and trustworthiness. It means stewarding our resources and responsibilities with integrity and excellence. It encompasses attitudes as well as actions.

Jesus said, "He who is faithful in what is least is faithful also in much; and he who is unjust in what is least is unjust also in much."[6]

Always remember, God is more concerned about character than achievements. In God's eyes, faithfulness is a far more precious commodity than natural talent, skills, intelligence, or spiritual gifts.

If I were assigned the task of choosing someone for such an important responsibility as fathering the nation of Israel, Abram would not have made it to my short list of potential candidates. I would seek out young, handsome, intelligent, muscular, virile men of excellent character. Once I narrowed down a group of young men who met these criteria, I'd have them undergo genetic testing to ensure they would propagate healthy children.

I definitely would not choose a relic like Abram; nor would I have selected his barren wife, Sarai, who was ninety years old when she finally gave birth to Isaac. Consider the dangers! Everyone knows that a woman's risk of bearing a child with mental or physical disabilities increases each year after the age of thirty-five.

God, unlike many of us, is utterly unimpressed by human prowess or talent. He treasures integrity, humility, faith, and faithfulness. That's not to say he doesn't value or use our talents—after all, he gave them to us—but he places much greater priority on character.

Abram proved his faithfulness time and again. Sure, he failed sometimes. He lied about his wife Sarai because of his fears. Then there was his really big-time blunder when, weary and discouraged after years of waiting for God to fulfill his promise, he came up with his own plan to make the vision come to pass. He and his wife decided that Abram would sleep with Sarai's maidservant in order to conceive a child. The plan worked (at least in their opinion) when Abram fathered Ishmael at the age of eighty-six.[7]

It's not that Abram stopped believing in the ultimate destiny God had promised him, but he took a shortcut. Relying on his own wisdom, he tried to make the dream happen in his own strength.

God's plan had always been that Abram would father a child through his wife, Sarai. Eventually, Abram repented of taking things into his own hands rather than waiting for God's perfect plan. Thirteen years after the birth of Ishmael, God appeared to Abram and reminded him of his covenant promise. He also changed Abram's name to Abraham, which literally means "father of many nations." He changed Sarai's name to Sarah, meaning "blessing." God affirmed that Abraham and Sarah would have a son, who would be named Isaac ("laughter"). This was the first time God revealed Isaac's name—yet another example of how God unfolds more details over time.

At the ripe old age of one hundred, Abraham experienced the fulfillment of God's promise when his son, Isaac, was finally born.[8]

Years later, the depth of Abraham's faith and character was poignantly revealed when God asked him to give up that precious son. Though he loved Isaac more than life itself, Abraham's obedience was instant, his trust unquestioning.

Of course, we know the end of the story—at the last moment the Lord appeared and stopped Abraham from sacrificing his son, saying, "Now I know that you fear God, because you have not withheld from me your son, your only son."[9]

Abraham's character had matured to the point that God could entrust anything to him. He could handle unlimited power, money, influence, and authority—for his heart was one hundred percent yielded to his Lord.

Many other examples in Scripture illustrate the value God places on a faithful, consecrated heart.

Take David, whom God chose to be king of Israel. After King Saul rebelled, God instructed the prophet Samuel to go to Jesse's household, where God would reveal which of Jesse's sons was chosen to be king.

Samuel was extremely impressed by Eliab. Not only was Eliab the tallest and most handsome of the sons, he also had considerable military experience—an important attribute for a king. Samuel thought to himself, "Surely the LORD's anointed stands here before the LORD."[10]

Wrong. God said to Samuel, "Do not consider his appearance or his height, for I have rejected him. The LORD does not look at the things man looks at. Man looks at the outward appearance, but the LORD looks at the heart."[11]

Outwardly, God's choice for a king was unimpressive. David was the youngest and smallest of the sons. A simple shepherd, David had never received military training like his brothers had. According to our human standards for assessing qualifications, David was a poor candidate for king. But David was God's choice. Later in the Bible, God described David as a man after his own heart.

In choosing the woman who would give birth to his son, Jesus, God never searched among the young women of nobility, for he was not seeking a woman renowned for her position in society or her personal talents or beauty. He chose Mary for her faith and character.

When the angel appeared to Mary to announce that the Holy Spirit would conceive in her and she would bear a son, the Messiah, she clearly understood the persecution she might suffer as a result. As an unmarried woman engaged to be married to Joseph, she risked losing Joseph and being shunned by society. Even so, Mary proved her consecration to God with her response: "I am the Lord's servant. . . . May it be to me as you have said."[12]

All of history's faith champions were men and women of faithfulness. None were perfect; most failed from time to time. All experienced moments of frustration. Most succumbed to doubt and unbelief from time to time. Many battled intense anxiety and fears, but they picked themselves up and pressed forward on their journey of faith.

The Next Step

One step at a time, one act of obedience at a time—that is how we are propelled forward on the pathway of purpose.

You will not receive revelation about the next leg of the pathway of purpose until you take the steps God is asking you to take now. Each act of obedience takes you closer to the next leg of the path. Each leg releases you into greater fulfillment of your destiny, but if you refuse to take the next step, you'll remain stuck in the same place on the path.

Faith is expressed through obedience. Often, God will direct us to do things that provoke feelings of intimidation or doubt. We may feel inferior to the task. The circumstances may seem impossible.

It's all too easy to justify disobedience when we feel fear or doubt. "I'm too shy." "That's just not my personality to do something like that." "I'm really under stress right now." These excuses will hinder us from reaching our dreams.

All of history's faith champions were men and women of faithfulness. None were perfect; most failed from time to time. All experienced moments of frustration. Most succumbed to doubt and unbelief from time to time. Many battled intense anxiety and fears, but they picked themselves up and pressed forward on their journey of faith.

Some people think they are being humble when they say, "I just can't do that." To the contrary, this attitude reflects pride, for it indicates they are trusting in themselves more than in God.

What steps has God asked you to take? Have you avoided taking them because of fear or doubt? If you wait for your feelings to change, you will never reach the next leg of your pathway of purpose.

Stepping out in faith will help you break free of your fears (see Chapter 11—*Conquering Fear*). You can be confident that as you obey God despite intimidation, he will lead you farther along the path of your destiny. As you walk each step of that path, he will progressively expand your vision, adding more clarity, focus, and details.

Human nature likes to have everything figured out. We would love to be able to see the entire picture, complete with a detailed road map. Trusting God means obeying him even when we don't understand the what, why, when, where, or how. It means trusting him with our future, confident that as we obey at each step, he will reveal additional vision and direction the moment we need to know it.

Our part in the process is simple: pray, listen, obey, and trust. For God to entrust us with greater vision, we must be faithful stewards of our present responsibilities.

A word of warning—if God is not directing you to take a new step right now, wait. Sometimes waiting is the hardest thing to do, but you can miss out on God's highest purpose if you take things into your own hands. Don't walk ahead of God, but don't walk behind him either. Just take the next step he has revealed to you, and you can be confident that he will lead you one step at a time along the pathway of your purpose.

Testing the Vision

As we grow in our relationship with God, it becomes easier to hear his voice, understand his will, and discern which desires harmonize with God's purposes for us.

It is sometimes hard to be sure of whether a dream is truly inspired by God or motivated by self-interest. Several practical biblical principles will help you test your passions and dreams. A vision inspired by God will have the following characteristics.

Consistency with Scripture

If you have a dream to marry your co-worker, who already has a wife, obviously you don't need to pray about whether this vision originates in God. God never contradicts his Word. He places such importance on the integrity of his Word that the Bible says, "You have exalted above all things your name and your word,"[13] and "The word of the Lord stands forever."[14] The Bible says of Jesus, "The Word became flesh."[15] Jesus said to his Father, "Your word is truth."[16]

This is such a basic principle it shouldn't need to be mentioned, but the sad reality is that many people claim God told them to do something that contradicts Scripture. In most cases, they are trying to justify their sin by spiritualizing it. This reflects a complete lack of reverence for God, for he will never lead us in a manner that contradicts his Word.

Inward Witness

One of the primary ways God guides us is through what many call the "inward witness." The Bible says, "The spirit of a man is the lamp of the LORD, Searching all the inner depths of his heart."[17]

When you pray about a particular vision, passion, or opportunity, what happens in your spirit? Do you experience an inward witness, a deep sense of peace? Or is there an unsettled feeling, a check, a warning? Have you truly brought your dream before God and bathed it in prayer, seeking his direction? Scripture also says, "The Spirit himself testifies with our spirit."[18]

Some people describe the inward witness as a "green light." I like that imagery. It can also be described as a harmonious, peaceful sense of "yes"—an inner awareness and certainty of resonating with God's purposes.

Contrast this with a "red light." This is often experienced as a warning, unease, unsettledness, or what some people call a "check."

As mentioned in a previous chapter, you can lose your sensitivity to the witness of the Holy Spirit if you habitually ignore his warnings and promptings. The only way to become more accurate in discerning the inner witness of the Spirit is to practise listening and obeying in everyday life.

The Bible says, "The peace of God, which transcends all understanding, will guard your hearts and your minds in Christ Jesus."[19]

A Prophetic Word

God may choose to speak to you through a prophet, but be careful you do not seek advice from prophets as your primary source of guidance. The Bible clearly states that we are to be directed by the Word of God and the Holy Spirit.

Prior to the death and resurrection of Jesus Christ, only certain spiritual leaders, such as the priests, prophets, and kings, received the Holy Spirit. Now everyone who is born again through Jesus Christ has the Holy Spirit in him or her. The apostle Paul reminds us, "Those who are led by the Spirit of God are sons of God."[20]

God may stir faith or conviction or bring about inner healing, direction, or edification through a prophetic word. It is unscriptural however, to depend on prophetic words from others more than you depend on the inner leading of the Holy Spirit.

If you do receive a prophetic word, the first test of its accuracy is that it will harmonize with Scripture. It will also bear witness in your spirit, confirming what God has already been revealing to you. You may not yet be consciously aware of what God has been trying to

102

convey to your spirit, especially if you are deeply wounded or not taking time to commune with God and receive from him. Nevertheless, if the prophecy is from God it will bear witness in your spirit.

Honouring to God

The vision will be pure, not self-seeking. Its greatest motivation will be to bring glory to Jesus Christ and to edify others.

The Bible says, "Whatever you do, do it all for the glory of God."[21]

As you continue to pray about your dream, your faith will increase, the dream will grow in intensity, and your relationship with God will deepen. Your dream will be accompanied by a greater desire and commitment to honour God in every area of your life.

Confirmed by Others

Has your vision been confirmed by others who are spiritually mature, know you well, and have proven qualities of wisdom, maturity, and discernment? Though you should not be looking for affirmation from everyone you know, it is important to seek counsel from spiritually mature individuals who know you well. The writer of Proverbs says, "Many advisers make victory sure."[22]

Willingness to Release It

If you are clutching your dream so tightly that you would do almost anything—even compromise—to fulfill your vision, it is time to release your hold. If your dream has become more important to you than your relationship with God, you are clinging too tightly. If you have no time to spend with God because you are too busy pursuing your dream, it has become an idol (an idol is anything that takes precedence over our relationship with God).

Paul the Apostle said, "I consider everything a loss compared to the surpassing greatness of knowing Christ Jesus my Lord, for whose sake I have lost all things."[23]

Surrender the dream to God. Yield ownership to him. This is not a one-time event but an ongoing process. We all succumb to spiritual idolatry from time to time; awareness of this tendency will help you remain humble and quick to repent when you go astray.

One of the warning signs that I have begun clutching my dreams too tightly is when I start feeling stressed out and anxious. For me, that is a red flag that I am holding on too tightly, that I have taken owner-ship of my dream or another area of my life. I immediately relinquish it back to its rightful owner, my heavenly Father. Peace follows instantly.

The Process

Some people hesitate to explore their dreams, all too aware of the areas in which they still need to change and grow. None of us, however, will experience perfection in this life. It's a process that will continue all our lives. If we were to wait until we became perfect to reach for our dreams, we would never accomplish one thing.

Al and Terri Purvis describe themselves as two simple farm kids who twenty years ago decided to follow the passion of their hearts to move to Thailand and establish a ministry that would help orphans and other hurting people. They left Canada with a few dol-lars and a dream to influence Asia—and embarked on the greatest adventure of their lives.

Once there, Al and Terri adopted thirty-one war orphans, form-ing the first El Shaddai Children's Home. They founded two addi-tional orphanages; established several churches and schools in Thailand, Pakistan, the Philippines, and Cambodia; founded an international Bible college in Thailand; and pioneered numerous outreach ministries in several countries. Two of their now-grown adopted children oversee orphanages and help many kids escape the sex trade. Many of their other grown children are in various posi-tions of leadership.

I heard Al tell their story in my church about a year ago.

"People often ask me how God called me to Thailand," Al said. "I don't know whether he ever did." He laughed. "At least not in the traditional way that people think of as a "call" from God. There was a deep passion in our hearts to go to Thailand and minister the love of God to hurting people. After taking that simple step of faith, it's amazing what God has done."

He continued, "God does speak, but I've found that he doesn't speak while you're sitting still doing nothing. If you will just step out and do what's in your heart, God will direct you. Just get moving. Do what God has placed in your heart to do, and he'll guide you."

As long as we desire to honour God, keeping our hearts humble and open, he is more than capable of adjusting our direction when necessary. Proverbs says, "Trust in the LORD with all your heart and lean not on your own understanding; in all your ways acknowledge him, and he will make your paths straight."[24]

Our job is simple: pray, listen, obey, and trust. David prayed, "Show me your ways, O LORD, teach me your paths; guide me in your truth and teach me."[25]

Take time daily to commune with God, attuning your spirit to be sensitive to his leading. Trust him to provide you with the direction you need at this time. Then, take the next step.

For Personal Reflection or Group Discussion

1. Do you feel the need to see far down the path, having all your ducks in a row, before you are willing to step out in faith?

2. Have you been waiting a long time for the fulfillment of a dream or a promise? What circumstances is God using in your life right now to prepare you for the future?

3. Would other people describe you as a faithful person? In the context of your current responsibilities, what does faithfulness mean to you?

4. What is the next step God is asking you to take? Will you commit to taking it?

Chapter Eight

Discerning Your Passions

Go confidently in the direction
of your dreams. Live the life
you have imagined.

Henry David Thoreau, *Walden*

For years, I grappled with the Bible verse, "Delight yourself in the LORD and he will give you the desires of your heart."[1] My relationship with God was performance oriented, and my interpretation of this Scripture verse went something like this: *If I serve God with all my heart, and rarely mess up, and continue to be faithful year after year after year—then maybe . . . someday . . . the time will come when God will reward me with my heart's desires.*

But, of course, I'm human and consistently fail to live up to my unrealistic standards. All too aware of my imperfections, I could never really trust this biblical promise.

Then one day, God corrected my misguided beliefs with a faith-inspiring revelation. I had set aside a full day in early January to pray and seek God's direction for the coming year. Though I pray daily for direction, at the beginning of each year I like to set aside a full day to seek God about longer-term goals. On this occasion, I received no direction for the first couple of hours, though I enjoyed the intimate presence of the Holy Spirit. Finally, God spoke to my heart: *What are your desires?*

I was taken aback by the question. *Lord,* I prayed, *I want to know what **your** desires are for me. I want to do your will.*

He repeated, *What are your desires?*

As I continued praying, he spoke to my spirit again: *Tap into your desires, and there you will find my purpose.*

I was stunned! Could it be possible my heart's desires harmonized with God's purpose for me?

For the first time, I truly comprehended—deep in my spirit, not just mentally—that God's promises were not based on my perfection. In fact, it was prideful for me to think I could ever earn his favour. God is looking for hearts that are humble before him, not perfect. I felt as though a huge weight was lifted from me.

One part of me felt like a kid in a candy store. *Really, God? You really, truly want to give me the desires of my heart?*

Another part of me felt a sobering sense of responsibility. If God trusted me with my desires, clearly the onus was on me to steward those desires. I had already developed some of my passions in my career and various ministries, but I had never taken the step of specifically defining my passions, writing them down, and holding myself accountable for developing them.

> *For the first time, I truly comprehended—deep in my spirit, not just mentally—that God's promises were not based on my perfection. In fact, it was prideful for me to think I could ever earn his favour. God is looking for hearts that are humble before him, not perfect. I felt as though a huge weight was lifted from me.*

As I began writing down the dreams of my heart, there were no real surprises. Some had been there since childhood. Take my passion to write. From the time I was a little girl, I wrote poems, songs, and stories. An ardent reader, I surrounded myself with stories, rushing home from school each day to enjoy a tryst with my beloved books. As an adult, I developed this desire through my writing career and ministry, but over time, as I grew in my relationship with God, the passion grew more focused and refined.

Then there was my entrepreneurial passion to pioneer new ventures, especially things that had never before been done. I explored that passion to some extent as a freelance journalist and later when I started my first business in corporate communications. I further developed the entrepreneurial gift when I helped my husband found and build a national citizen action organization. We started with nothing but a vision in our hearts, but through God's power and grace built something that is having a powerful impact on the nation of Canada.

One of my latest entrepreneurial ventures is an on-line women's magazine called LifeToolsforWomen.com, with a mission to inspire and equip women around the world to reach their divine potential through a relationship with Jesus Christ.

And who knows—God may direct me to pioneer many more ventures in the future. I'm confident that as long as I steward the vision God gives me at each step of my journey, he will continue to guide me into greater effectiveness and fruitfulness.

One passion that God uncovered over time—and which I was completely oblivious to—was speaking and teaching. My greatest fear at one time was public speaking. Never in a million years would I have imagined that I might come alive with faith and anointing when teaching. This is an example of a passion that was unveiled as God set me free from fear.

As I continued searching my heart, other desires came to light. Some were buried under the clutter and busyness of life. Others had been enshrouded by doubt and unbelief. It was time to unearth those desires from their hiding places.

Still other desires came to mind that I knew were simply not "in season." Anyone who has spent time in Canada knows that even the most talented horticulturalist will never grow roses in a Canadian winter, unless, of course, she has a greenhouse. Even then, the roses won't thrive. Likewise, there are seasons for being released into our gifts and callings. We need to continually pray for discernment so we do not become frustrated trying to grow roses in winter.

Patience is crucial as we pursue our passions and dreams. To prepare us for each new level of purpose, God leads us on a journey of character development. Sometimes that journey may seem as though it is taking forever. Still, it is vital to avoid the temptation to try to short-circuit the work God wants to do in our hearts.

Unveiling Your Passions

To unveil the deepest passions of your heart, you may need to lift up some shrouds that have covered them.

Voices of fear, doubt, cynicism, inferiority, and other deeply ingrained negative thought patterns and emotional attitudes drown out the gentle whisper of holy passion. Over time, your truest heart passions may be silenced.

You may have developed a habit of thinking within the box, your belief system limited by circumstances, your past, or your own abilities. Perhaps you interpret life through the message of the boxes.

Patience is crucial as we pursue our passions and dreams. To prepare us for each new level of purpose, God leads us on a journey of character development. Sometimes that journey may seem as though it is taking forever. Still, it is vital to avoid the temptation to try to short-circuit the work God wants to do in our hearts.

Thinking within the box traps our potential, which is why the Bible exhorts us to renew our minds with the Word of God. If we commit ourselves to ongoing spiritual development, God creates new thought patterns in our minds. We become possibility thinkers, envisioning great dreams and believing in God's miracle-working power to fulfill them.

Using your gifts in service to God should bring joy, not misery. If you dread going to work each day, if your ministry is pure drudgery, if the only thing that you look forward to is sitting in front of the television watching your favourite sitcom or fantasizing about your future retirement—you have no vision of your calling. You are not honouring your raw material.

If what you are now doing inspires no joy or vision, it is highly improbable that you are following your divinely ordained mission. As Laurie Beth Jones says in *The Path*, "Bees hum when they work—they don't whine."

What makes you hum? What makes your heart sing? What excites and motivates you? What produces a deep inner assurance that this is what you were born to do?

Serving in your calling should stir passion, joy, and faith. You will notice what the Psalmist declares, "I desire to do your will, O my God."[2]

When our spirits come alive through a relationship with Jesus Christ, the Holy Spirit ignites a longing for purpose. As we grow spiritually, fuel is added to that flame until it burns with such intense heat that we will become increasingly uncomfortable until we do something about it.

John Ortberg says in *If You Want to Walk on Water You've Got to Get Out of the Boat,*

> As a crucial part of your calling, you were given certain gifts, talents, longings, and desires. To identify these with clarity, to develop them with skill, and to use them joyfully and humbly to serve God and his creation is central to why you were created.[3]

Destiny, gifts, and passions are inextricably linked, and the truest evidence of a gifting is a passion for it.

Remember, God sees unlimited potential in you. He sees impossible dreams coming to pass through his power and grace working through you. When he looks at you, he envisions the woman or man you can become through his transforming power.

Invite God to probe the deepest places of your heart to unveil divine dreams and passions buried under the shrouds of inferiority, unbelief, self-doubt, and fear. Pray for revelation of what he wants to do through your life—which is so much greater than anything you could conceive on your own. Pray that he will teach you to become a "possibility thinker" who dreams big and walks by faith.

If you truly desire to honour God, he will lead you. You can trust him with your most cherished dreams and desires. Over time, you will gain greater clarity of God's purpose for those passions. Your purpose will be a perfect fit for you. It will harmonize with the gifts, passions, personality, and spiritual gifts that God placed in you.

Remember, God sees unlimited potential in you. He sees impossible dreams coming to pass through his power and grace working through you. When he looks at you, he envisions the woman or man you can become through his transforming power.

Identifying Your Passions

Before you can explore your passions, you must identify them. Once you have lifted the veils, gaze upon the naked desires of your heart and do something tangible to acknowledge them—you may want to speak them out loud, write them down, or tell a trusted friend. Most importantly, acknowledge your desires to God (this is for your benefit, not his). You may feel timid at first, especially if you have been listening to the message of the boxes all your life. Be prepared for thoughts such as, *What if I miss God? What would people think? I'll be so embarrassed if I fail.*

You started this process in Chapter 2. Hopefully you have been flexing your dreaming muscles by scheduling regular times to freely ponder and write about your desires. Now is the time to revisit that list. Go deeper. Tap into the rivers of your heart and see where they naturally flow. Search your heart and answer these questions:

- What inspires creativity, ideas and vision in me?
- What do I desire to do more than anything else?
- What stirs joy in my heart?
- Is there anything that excites me so much that I sometimes lie awake at night thinking about it?
- What is it about the world or about human suffering that makes me angry and spurs me to want to do something?
- What are my life messages? (Life messages are experiences and themes that you are passionate about sharing with others.)
- If there were absolutely no constraints (time, money, skills, resources, etc.) and I could do anything, what would it be?

It may help you to define your passions by thinking about people you would like to help. For example, do you have a special compassion for homeless people, unwed mothers, new immigrants, or troubled teens?

Another aid to defining passion is to think about arenas in which you would like to make a difference. Your passion may relate to issues that you want to change—for example, poverty, the education system, politics, or unemployment. It may relate to the arts—you may be passionate about singing, playing an instrument, painting, or drama. It may relate to entrepreneurial ventures; perhaps you would love to pioneer a new ministry, business, or other venture.

Clues to your passions also may be found by recollecting what you loved doing as a child. Take a trip back in time, and think about the things that interested you most when you were young. Were you intrigued by gardening, building sandcastles, reading, writing, drawing, acting, nurturing, teaching, or bossing others around (often a sign of leadership and administrative skills)? Explore those desires and pray about how they relate to your life calling.

One woman I know, whose ministry is speaking at women's conferences and seminars, recalls playing "preacher" as early as the age of three. She used to set up a dozen or so chairs in her basement and seat all of her dolls and teddy bears in the chairs. Then she would grab a toy microphone and "preach" to her audience, followed by prayer for each one. Today, she is living that passion (though with people, of course).

When my brother, Ken, was a child, he and our youngest sister often baked cakes together. Actually, Ken gave the orders and Dianne baked the cakes. Ken would "share the vision"—how wonderful it would be to eat a luscious chocolate cake dripping in rich, gooey icing. Then he would read the instructions in the recipe to Dianne, supervising each step along the way. He even convinced her to wash the dishes. (Somehow, Dianne never figured out that she was doing all the work.) Today, Ken is the president and CEO of a successful corporation, and one of his greatest strengths is imparting vision.

My niece, Karalee, was telling jokes and acting when she was two years old. By the time she was five, she was earning an impressive income acting in television commercials for toy companies. Later, she won top roles in school and church drama productions, and was often asked to speak at school functions. Today, she is enrolled in broadcast journalism and cinema arts at college, further developing the passion that has been evident since she was toddler.

Having said that clues to your calling may be found in your past, *never* conclude that your past is the primary factor in defining your future. Many children are raised in such dysfunctional circumstances that they never have the opportunity to connect with the desires of their hearts. Often, when these children grow to adulthood, they have no conscious memories of childhood desires or dreams.

The wonderful message of redemption triumphs over every other life message. Jesus has promised to reclaim our spiritual birthright from the clutches of Satan, sin, and circumstances. He restores purpose from the inside out. You are *not* a prisoner to your past.

By far the most important way you can tap into your passions is to draw closer to Jesus. After all, God made you; he is the one who planted the seeds of potential in your heart. Regardless of how deep those seeds are buried or how often they have been trampled on through the years, his resurrection power can release them to grow and blossom. There is no right or wrong passion, as long as you desire to honour God and edify others.

Ask God to illuminate the passions he placed in your heart. Ask him to unearth divine dreams that may be buried under the rubble of disappointment and failure. Trust him to walk with you and help you remove the shrouds that have veiled your desires. Trust him to show you how to respond to the inner yearning to find and fulfill your destiny.

In the previous chapter, we discussed how vision unfolds progressively as we grow in our relationship with God and as we obey him each step along the way. Discerning your passions is also a journey. For some, it comes easily. For others, it takes considerable time.

Be patient. God is faithful. Over time, he will lead you into deeper and more focused understanding of your passions and gifts.

Trying Something New

Benjamin Franklin said, "Hide not your talents, they for use were made. What use is a sundial in the shade?"

God has graciously endowed each of us with natural talents and spiritual gifts; it is incumbent upon us to steward them to the best of our ability. We are born with natural talents and abilities, and we receive spiritual gifts when we are born again through Jesus Christ.

The apostle Peter says,

As each of you has received a gift (a particular spiritual talent, a gracious divine endowment), employ it for one another as

114

[befits] good trustees of God's many-sided grace [faithful stewards of the extremely diverse powers and gifts granted to Christians by unmerited favor].[4]

One of the best ways of discovering your passions, abilities, and spiritual gifts is to try new things. You may have heard the adage, "God can steer a moving vehicle, but he can't move one that is stationary." The time to step out and explore your passions is now. Not tomorrow. Not next year. Not in five years when you think you will be more spiritually mature.

If Al and Terry Purvis had waited until they were older, more experienced, more skilled, more educated, or more spiritual—they may have never made it to Thailand. They stepped out in faith, and God did the rest.

Experiment. Try something you have never done before. Observe what happens in you. Did you feel more alive? Were you inspired with creative ideas and vision? Were you excited? Did your friends or family comment that they hadn't seen you so motivated about something in a long time? Did you experience a deep, abiding faith that you were in the centre of God's will? Did that faith remain even when facing discouragement and seemingly insurmountable obstacles? Did you draw closer to God? Did you feel a deep sense of gratitude to God? Was there a sense of resonating with divine purpose, that you were doing the very thing you were born to do?

"You have dozens of hidden abilities and gifts you don't know you've got because you've never tried them out," says Rick Warren in *The Purpose Driven Life.*

No matter how old you are, I urge you to never stop experimenting. I know a woman in her nineties who runs and wins 10K races and didn't discover that she enjoyed running until she was seventy-eight![5]

Our friend Abby is a social worker. Though she enjoyed her profession, after a few years she became bored, feeling as though she wasn't making much of a contribution. She prayed that God would show her how she could make a difference. She began to feel a special compassion for the challenges faced by new immigrants, and she began to envision ways she could help them make an easier transition to our culture.

Abby presented her idea to her employer and obtained permission for a trial project, which was an outstanding success. Abby discovered previously untapped reservoirs of passion and enthusiasm, and she had the satisfaction of knowing she was truly making a difference. The program was so successful that her employer quadrupled her budget so she could hire more staff and expand the program throughout the city.

Jason discovered a passion and gift for helping children from single-parent families by first volunteering to teach in his church's Sunday school. Though he enjoyed teaching his class, he didn't feel particularly passionate about it, nor did he feel he was making much of a difference. As he continued teaching the class, he found himself especially drawn to kids who had lost a parent to death or divorce. He started a new ministry to provide support for those kids. Not only is he making a powerful difference in the lives of these children, he feels he is doing the very thing he was born to do. But Jason may have never discovered that passion if he hadn't tried something new and volunteered to teach Sunday school.

Remember, diving into the river of desire is most of all an act of faith. Faith doesn't mean having all your ducks in a row. It just means taking the next step. Steward what God has revealed to you thus far on your journey. Explore your gifts and passions. As you do, those passions will become more clearly defined, and you will develop a broader and more specific vision of how they fit with your purpose.

If you have a desire to be involved in the business arena, don't sit around and wait for someone to offer you the chairmanship of a Fortune 500 company. Take some business courses. Seek out successful business people as your mentors. Get advice from others. Learn everything you can and pursue opportunities. Trust God's promise to guide you.

If you have a desire to teach children, consider volunteering in a local community project that helps teach life skills to disadvantaged children. Thousands of non-profit agencies are looking for teaching volunteers. Or teach in your church's Sunday school.

Perhaps you believe you have a gift to teach the Bible. If so, study Scripture. Study some more. Take Bible courses. Listen to recorded messages of spiritually mature speakers. Don't turn your nose up when the only opportunities you receive at first are teaching classes of three-year-olds in Sunday school.

Remember this: in everything you do, God will be testing your motives and attitudes. Pursue excellence. If you have a vision to conduct business management seminars to large groups of business leaders, but the only audience available to you is a classroom of rambunctious fourth-graders, pour your talents into them with the same passion and commitment that you would if you were addressing an audience of thousands.

I know some people whose commitment level plunges when they are doing volunteer work or if they are not receiving the recognition they think they deserve. That attitude is a stench to God. The apostle Paul reminds us, "And whatever you do, whether in word or deed, do it all in the name of the Lord Jesus, giving thanks to God the Father through him."[6]

If you make a commitment to do something, do it with the same dedication and zeal as if you were receiving thousands of dollars an hour or were being broadcast on national television. Anything less reflects pride and self-seeking motives. God will always test you in small things before releasing you into bigger things.

In summary, try something new. Explore your passions. Experiment. If you truly desire God's will, you can trust him to adjust your direction if you get off track. And whatever you do, do it with all your heart and with a commitment to excellence. As you step out to develop your gifts and serve others, continually praying for God's guidance, he will provide increasingly greater clarity of your passions and purpose.

Remember, diving into the river of desire is most of all an act of faith. Faith doesn't mean having all your ducks in a row. It just means taking the next step. Steward what God has revealed to you thus far on your journey. Explore your gifts and passions. As you do, those passions will become more clearly defined, and you will develop a broader and more specific vision of how they fit with your purpose.

For Personal Reflection or Group Discussion

1. Do you tend to be excessively analytical, hesitant to step out and do anything unless you are one hundred percent certain of God's leading? How has this held you back?

2. Reread the questions in this chapter's section "Identifying Your Passions." Take time to really search your heart and write down everything that comes to mind. What new things did you discover about yourself?

3. Is there anything you loved to do as a child that is evidenced in a passion you still have today?

4. Can you think of an example of something new that you tried that unveiled a previously hidden passion or talent?

Chapter Nine

Defining Mission, Vision, and Goals

Goals are dreams with deadlines.

Diana Scharf Hunt

A leading business consultant who provides training to top corporate executives begins each session with a quiz; the first question is "What is your corporation's mission statement?" In more than ninety percent of cases, not one person—not even the CEO or president—can state the corporate mission.

Last year I attended a seminar where the attendees were asked to define their personal mission or purpose in one sentence. Out of a group of about three hundred people, fewer than a dozen were able to articulate a purpose statement.

It's not that living with purpose is a low priority for most of us. Research by Richard J. Leider and David Shapiro, authors of *Repacking Your Bags*, found that the number one deadly fear of most people is "having lived a meaningless life."

Why, then, does writing a mission statement seem like such a daunting task?

I believe the main reason lies in the lack of practical resources. Though you can avail yourself of prolific advice about writing mission

119

statements from management experts, books, the Internet, and so forth, most of this information is complex and confusing. Most of these resources target corporations and organizations, providing little practical advice for an individual who wants to craft a personal mission statement.

Another reason many people hesitate to articulate a mission statement is they are worried about not achieving one hundred percent accuracy in discerning their purpose (especially Christians and recovering perfectionists like me). Time and again people have told me they are afraid of misinterpreting God's will. They say things like "How can I be sure I'm accurately discerning God's purposes? Isn't it presumptuous to write out my own plan? How does planning allow for divine intervention?"

Remember, vision unfolds progressively. If you wait to set goals until you see the entire picture, you will wait forever.

Among countless other Scriptures assuring us of divine guidance, God promises, "I will instruct you and teach you in the way you should go; I will counsel you and watch over you."[1]

Don't fret about whether you perfectly define your purpose. If you keep your heart right and truly desire God's best, you can trust God to adjust your path if you are getting off track. As Proverbs tells us, "In his heart a man plans his course, but the LORD determines his steps."[2]

Finally, many people do not realize the power unleashed through the simple act of writing out their vision. Vague, undefined ideas that lack clarity and specifics rarely translate into reality.

When you were a child, you probably learned how to start a fire by focusing sunlight through a magnifying glass. Sunlight alone could not start the fire; it had to be focused through the magnifying glass. This reflects a basic principle of solar energy—though a large amount of sunlight falls on the earth, the light is diffused. For the sun to be utilized for heating, solar energy units must be designed to collect and concentrate the light.

The same principle applies to purpose. It must be focused to produce results. With no focus, there is no mechanism for establishing direction or goals.

The Bible says, "Write the vision and make it plain on tablets, That he may run who reads it."[3] The simple act of writing your vision is a powerful catalyst for launching you into your destiny. It keeps you focused, helps you establish priorities, and propels you to action.

Committing yourself to defining your purpose is perhaps the most important task you could ever engage in. "Discovering your purpose will put your life into crystal-clear perspective," says Mark Victor Hansen in an on-line article, "Conceptualize your Purpose." "You will see another world, one in which you are a necessary and intricate spoke in the wheel."

Don't fret about whether you perfectly define your purpose. If you keep your heart right and truly desire God's best, you can trust God to adjust your path if you are getting off track. As Proverbs tells us, "In his heart a man plans his course, but the LORD determines his steps."

In previous chapters, we discussed principles for discerning divinely inspired passions and dreams. Now you are ready to take the all-important step of articulating and writing a purpose statement.

Your Personal Mission Statement

What is a mission statement?

Since this book focuses on personal life purpose, as opposed to a corporate or organizational purpose, I'm going to simplify the process with the aim of making it easy for individuals who desire to articulate their purpose.

"The more elaborate it is, the less likely it is understood and remembered," says business-life coach Barbara McRae in her article "The Top 10 Keys to Crafting a Compelling Mission Statement."

Even if you lead a company, ministry, or organization, it is vital that you start with your personal mission before adapting these principles to your corporation or organization. Let's use the following definitions:

Mission Statement: Concise statement of your life purpose.

Vision Statement: Concise statement of the unique and distinctive ways that you will accomplish your purpose.

Action Plan: Specific goals for achieving your vision statement.

The first place to start is your mission statement. I will use the terms *mission* and *purpose* interchangeably. Choose the term you like best.

Think of your mission statement as a general statement encompassing your reason for existence—in other words, a broad statement of what you hope to accomplish. It does *not* include the distinctive ways that you intend to accomplish your purpose; that will be articulated in your vision statement.

Your mission statement will help you stay on course. In *First Things First*, Stephen Covey emphasizes the motivation and energy that result from an effective mission statement.

> What we're talking about here is not simply writing a statement of belief. We're talking about accessing and creating an open connection with the deep energy that comes from a well-defined, thoroughly integrated sense of purpose and meaning in life. We're talking about creating a powerful vision based on the true north principles that ensure its achievability. We're talking about the sense of excitement and adventure that grows out of connecting with your unique purpose and the profound satisfaction that comes in fulfilling it.[4]

Before you develop your mission statement, it is important to understand what a mission statement is *not*. It is not a to-do list. Nor is it a statement of strategies or methods. It is not a job description. Jobs and roles change through life's seasons; purpose embodies a broad vision that encompasses all your roles.

Over time, your mission statement will become more refined. As you grow in your relationship with God, revelation of your calling will also become more specific and focused. This does not mean your purpose has changed; it simply means that you have acquired clearer revelation of your purpose.

You may not see a clear picture right now, and that's fine. Relax. Don't sweat it. Enjoy the process. After all, you can define your mission only within the context of what God has revealed to you at this point on your spiritual journey. He will paint in more details, colours, and shapes as time goes on.

In other words, your mission statement is not written in stone. You can and should revisit it periodically. Most likely, you will revise and fine-tune it time and again. Don't be concerned about whether it is precisely accurate. Trust the Holy Spirit to lead you in this endeavour.

Take time out from your busy schedule to prayerfully reflect on your personal mission, as you understand it at this point on your journey. Look at the big picture, and ask yourself questions like, *Who am I? Why am I here? What are my desires and dreams? What is my mission, or purpose?*

Defining your purpose should be a stimulating and motivating exercise. It should stir enthusiasm and excitement.

Many people feel that purpose must relate to a vision of achieving something of great magnitude or something that affects a nation or even the entire world. But purpose does not necessarily involve grandiose ideas.

I like what Dr. Martin Luther King Jr. said: "Everyone has the power for greatness—not for fame but greatness, because greatness is determined by service."

Avoid measuring the value of purpose based on how many people it will have an impact on or how much recognition you will receive. God has not called you to be Mother Teresa or Billy Graham or Margaret Thatcher; he has called you to be you. Nothing more. Nothing less.

If you are faithful to do your best to develop your gifts and achieve your purpose, you will make an impact for eternity, whether you realize it in this life or not. Simply commit to honouring and stewarding the specific call and raw material God has placed in you.

Defining your passions within a larger context will help you articulate your purpose.

Successful people have a clear vision of not only what they want to do but also why. The *why* is as important as the *what,* for it is the *why* that fuels vision and keeps you motivated when you face setbacks.

Divine purpose springs from a sincere motivation to honour God, serve others, and make the world a better place. Desires contaminated by selfish ambition and pride never blossom into the fullness of their intended purpose, even if those desires originate in God. Our gifts and dreams were designed for a far greater purpose than to simply make us happy.

Having said that, joy and contentment are by-products of using your gifts to serve God and others.

On a practical level, understanding *why* you want to do something will help you define your purpose. For example, perhaps you believe you are called to leadership in the business arena. Ask yourself, *Why do I want to do this?*

If your only motivation is to make lots of money and buy more things, then you have not yet discerned your purpose. You may indeed have God-given leadership abilities, but those gifts were meant for a far greater purpose than merely accumulating more stuff.

Ask God to help you understand how you can use your gifts to serve others. Always seek revelation of the broad purpose for the gifts and passions he has placed in your heart.

Divine purpose springs from a sincere motivation to honour God, serve others, and make the world a better place. Desires contaminated by selfish ambition and pride never blossom into the fullness of their intended purpose, even if those desires originate in God. Our gifts and dreams were designed for a far greater purpose than to simply make us happy.

Now get out some paper or your Palm Pilot or laptop or whatever communications gadget you like best, and begin drafting your mission statement. I'll say it again—*do not obsess about getting it perfect*. I wrote and rewrote my mission statement many times before I felt it accurately reflected what God placed in my heart. And who knows, I may refine it again in the future.

Keep revising it until you can define it in one clear, concise sentence.

Here is my mission statement: "To inspire and equip women to reach their divine potential."

Notice that this statement does not include the specifics of *how* I will accomplish my mission. It says nothing about the unique and distinctive strategies I will employ for achieving my purpose.

Here are a few examples of what I consider to be excellent mission statements:

"To recognize, inspire, and promote divine connection in myself and others"—Laurie Beth Jones, best-selling author, speaker, and consultant.

"To help as many people as I can during my lifetime, in a way that significantly improves their lives"—Les Hewitt, best-selling author and business coach.

"To inspire and empower people to live their highest vision in a context of love and joy"—Jack Canfield, co-author of the outrageously successful *Chicken Soup for the Soul* series of books.

From these examples, you can see that an effective mission statement is not a job description—it is a clear, inspiring, engaging statement of your broad life mission.

Your Vision Statement

Now that you have defined your mission statement in one sentence, you are ready to take the next step and craft your vision statement. The vision statement adds the all-important *how*. It defines the distinctive and specific ways that you will accomplish your mission.

George Barna says in *The Power of Vision*, "While the mission statement is philosophic in nature, the vision statement is strategic in nature." While mission relates to general approaches, "vision relates to specific actions."[5]

Your vision statement propels your mission to specific strategies. Specifying the primary activities you will pursue to accomplish your purpose, it reflects your unique passions, talents, and skills.

You should be able to define your vision statement in one concise paragraph. The first sentence of this paragraph is your mission statement. The next one or two sentences specify *how* you will accomplish your mission.

Your vision statement will evolve over time, reflecting your ongoing spiritual growth, character development, and the acquisition of more skills and experience.

At one time, my vision statement read as follows: "To inspire and equip women to reach their divine potential. This will be accomplished by writing articles and books and by speaking at conferences and seminars."

As time went on, I revised my vision statement to the following:

To inspire and equip women to reach their divine potential.
This will be accomplished by writing articles, columns, books,

and e-books; by publishing an on-line women's magazine; and by speaking at conferences and seminars.

Notice that the first sentence (my mission statement) did not change. The next sentence, which encompasses *how* I will achieve my mission, continues evolving as God unfolds more vision, as I grow spiritually, and as I acquire additional skills and experience.

Thousands of other women may have the same mission statement as mine but different vision statements reflecting their unique gifts and callings.

For example, one woman might reach the same mission as mine through counselling. Her vision statement might read something like this: "To inspire and equip women to reach their divine potential. This will be accomplished through personal counselling."

Another woman might have a vision statement like this: "To inspire and equip women to reach their divine potential. This will be accomplished by coaching women in leadership and business management skills."

Can you see how the vision statement encompasses uniqueness and specificity? It is the vision statement—not the mission statement—that reflects your unique gifts and strategies.

Your vision statement serves as a compass to keep things going in the right direction. It helps you measure your progress, set goals, establish priorities, and know when to use one of the most important words in your vocabulary: *No.*

One of my favourite movies is *Apollo 13.* I never fail to be inspired by the courage and resourcefulness of the astronauts amid unimaginable pressure and seemingly impossible odds. On top of a litany of other crippling technical problems, the astronauts were faced with the reality that their oxygen could run out, they could be poisoned by carbon dioxide accumulations, or they could freeze to death. Even if they managed to return to the earth's atmosphere, they had to enter at precisely the right angle.

If you've seen the movie, you'll recall there were many decisions and actions that contributed to their successful landing. One of those actions was ensuring they kept the earth in sight at all times, for they had lost their navigational equipment.

In the same way, your vision statement will keep you moving in the right direction. It will help you stay focused on the big picture, even when facing emotional upheaval, discouragement, obstacles, and all the other distractions that life throws at you.

Your Action Plan

Mission and vision statements provide focus to your purpose. Your action plan involves setting specific goals for accomplishing your purpose. Goals represent specific, measurable actions. With no goals, your mission and vision statements will go no further than the paper you wrote them on.

"In the long run men only hit what they aim for," said Henry David Thoreau.

Goals put feet to your vision. As the Bible says, "Faith by itself, if it is not accompanied by action, is dead."[6] You may have great dreams and vision, but if you don't translate that vision into tangible goals, you will never see any results.

"Setting and achieving goals is one of the best ways to measure your life's progress and create unusual clarity," say Jack Canfield, Mark Victor Hansen, and Les Hewitt.

Consider the alternative—just drifting along aimlessly, hoping that one day good fortune will fall into your lap with little or no effort on your part. Wake up! You've got more chance of finding a grain of sugar on a sandy beach.[7]

Think of your goals as tools for achieving your purpose. They focus your vision into tangible actions.

Many people go through life accomplishing nothing because they never set goals. They may talk to anyone who will listen about their wonderful vision, exciting dreams, creative ideas, and grandiose plans—but they spend their life running around in circles, expending huge amounts of energy and never going anywhere.

"The reason most people never reach their goals is that they don't define them, or ever seriously consider them as believable or achievable," says author, lecturer, and productivity consultant Denis Waitley.

"Winners can tell you where they are going, what they plan to do along the way, and who will be sharing the adventure with them."

Following are characteristics of effective goals.

Specific and Measurable

A goal is a target, not a vague generalization. It must be specific and include some way of measuring progress. If you haven't stated a specific destination, how will you know when you get there?

For example, let's say you want to lose weight and improve your general health. This is a commendable plan, but it is not a goal. First, it is too general. Second, there is no way to measure it. How will you know when you have achieved it?

You could translate your vision into two specific goals, as follows:

Goal 1: Lose thirty pounds by the end of the year by cutting down on fat, starches, and sugars.

Goal 2: Exercise aerobically four times a week for thirty-five minutes.

Both these goals provide a specific target to work toward. By providing practical, clearly defined direction, they propel you to action. It is one thing to say you want to lose weight. By stating your goal to lose thirty pounds within a specific time frame, you will be able to measure your progress, and by including the specific means for reaching your goal, you provide tangible, doable, practical actions you can apply on a daily basis.

"Setting and achieving goals is one of the best ways to measure your life's progress and create unusual clarity," say Jack Canfield, Mark Victor Hansen, and Les Hewitt. "Consider the alternative—just drifting along aimlessly, hoping that one day good fortune will fall into your lap with little or no effort on your part. Wake up! You've got more chance of finding a grain of sugar on a sandy beach."[7]

Let's look at another example of how a vision can be translated into tangible goals. Perhaps you have a dream to build a successful Internet marketing business. Following are examples of goals that would help you put legs to your vision:

One-year goal: Launch Internet marketing business.

Nine-month goal: Complete business plan.

Six-month goal: Read at least six books on Internet marketing.

Three-month goal: Meet with several individuals with expertise in Internet marketing for advice and input.

One-month goals: Read two books on Internet marketing; subscribe to twelve Internet marketing e-newsletters; meet with business coach and start business planning process.

One-week goals: Order Internet marketing books; research Internet marketing newsletters.

Of course, you will need many more goals than these to build your business, but these examples illustrate the process for translating vision into specific, measurable goals.

Keep your vision statement before you constantly to ensure your goals reflect your overall purpose. It's important to review them periodically and ask, *Are these goals propelling me toward my purpose?*

If you're like most people, there are many good things you could be doing with your time. The question is, do they reflect the *best* use of your time? Goals, defined within the context of your vision statement, will help you prioritize. Many people fill their to-do lists with things that they believe are urgent, but there is a big difference between the urgent and the important. Learn to distinguish between the two.

Flexible

Your goals will change as your vision expands. By stating specific goals, you have a method for continually evaluating your progress. When you reach one goal, it's time to set another.

Be careful to avoid making your goals more important than your vision. Goals do not comprise your purpose; they are *tools* for accomplishing your purpose. Always keep the big picture before you. Review your vision statement on a regular basis, and be open to God stretching your faith and your vision, which of course will result in new goals over time.

When I launched my on-line women's magazine—LifetoolsforWomen.com—my one-year goal was to have 5,000 monthly visitors by the end of the first year, reading about 10,000 pages. That was definitely a "faith goal" for me, as I didn't invest any money in marketing and promotion; nor did I have much time to devote to this project. Only God could bring this to pass.

Thirteen months later, the magazine reached 5,300 monthly visitors, reading just under 11,000 pages! I was thrilled. I certainly couldn't take any credit. Several "experts" had told me that my one-year goal was unrealistic and impossible without a substantial investment in marketing.

Meanwhile, during that first year of building the magazine, my faith and vision also grew. Though 5,000 monthly visitors seemed like a monstrous goal when I launched the magazine, two years later, my vision had grown to reach 300,000 monthly visitors within five years, reading 500,000 pages. In just the past year (the second year), monthly visitors and the number of pages viewed each month tripled (and I still haven't invested anything in formal marketing). My heart burns with a passion to reach women around the world, inspiring them with a vision of the purpose and potential that can unfold through a relationship with Jesus Christ.

Do you see how vision expands and becomes more focused and detailed as we steward the vision we have already received? There is no way I could have embraced goals of this magnitude when I first started this magazine. My vision expanded as I simply took each step God instructed me to take.

With each step of faith and obedience, God opens new doors of impossibility in our hearts.

God loves big dreams. I believe he is insulted by small dreams and easy-to-reach goals, for we can accomplish those on our own. He likes dreams that require total dependence on him.

Realistic

Having just said that we need to set goals that require divine intervention, we must also be realistic. In other words, your goals should reflect the raw material God has placed in you. If you can't even carry a tune, there's little point in setting a goal to become an internationally renowned soloist.

Again, think about who *you* are. Don't set goals because you think other people will admire you for achieving those goals. Avoid comparing yourself to others. Discern the passions that God has placed in *your* heart. Your true heart passions will reflect the raw material that God has placed in you.

One factor involved in evaluating whether or not your goals are realistic is to answer the question, *Is my goal feasible?*

For example, if your goal is to be fully self-employed in one month but you haven't even started your new business, let alone developed it to where it is producing revenue, and you have a family to support, your goal is clearly unrealistic (not to mention foolish).

Another question to ask is, *Am I willing to pay the price and work toward my goal?* Perhaps you have a goal to teach courses at a Bible college in one year, but you rarely study the Bible, have never taken Bible courses yourself, and have no experience teaching. Clearly, your goal is unrealistic (and unattainable if you are not willing to prepare yourself).

Also, take into consideration the time necessary to acquire skills and experience. If you have never worked in the financial arena but have set a goal to obtain a position as vice-president of finance for a major corporation within one year, well, clearly the timing needs adjusting. The skills and expertise required to go from where you are to where you want to be cannot be acquired in that short a time frame.

In setting goals, be realistic about your efficiency. For many years, I habitually set unrealistic goals, based on the assumption that I would work at one hundred percent efficiency one hundred and ten percent of the time. In real life, that never happened. Some days I was sick. Some days I was exhausted and not as productive. And some days God had other priorities for me that had nothing to do with my goals, such as visiting a lonely friend or simply taking time off to relax.

In addition to these practical principles for evaluating whether or not your goal is realistic, measure your goal in light of your faith. Do you truly have faith for your dream? I'm not talking about pie-in-the-sky desires or hopeful fantasies but that deep, abiding faith that grows the more you pray about it and the more you work toward it. This is the kind of faith that won't lose its grip on your heart—even during those times when you are overwhelmed by discouragement and want to run away from your dream. The New Testament says, "faith is the substance of things hoped for."[8]

Balanced

Researchers asked a large group of elderly people what they would do differently if they could start life all over again. Less than five percent said they would like to make more money. Most said they would take more time for family, relationships, travel, and enjoying the simple pleasures of life.

Goals must be balanced. Visionaries are especially prone to imbalance in their personal lives.

There are benefits to being focused, of course, but it can also work against us if we are not intentional about maintaining balance. As an intensely vision-oriented person, I have had to really work on this area.

The most important key to balance is self-awareness—to know your weak areas and recognize the warning signs when your life is becoming unbalanced. If you focus all of your time, effort, money, and talents on your dream, rarely taking time for relationships or recreation, you will be discontent and frustrated. Eventually you will burn out.

If you have a tendency to neglect your personal life, it is important to set goals in this area in the same way you set goals for your work or ministry.

Time off is important, regardless of whether you think you need it or not. I am far more productive Monday through Friday if I do absolutely nothing relating to work on the weekends, unless it is an emergency. Because my office is located in my home, sometimes I have to fight the temptation to check my e-mail on the weekend.

My husband and I have learned that a mental break is even more important than a physical break. For that reason, we never check phone messages or e-mail relating to work when on vacation. If possible, we try to leave the country, and once we embark on the airplane, we leave everything behind. We focus on God, nature, our relationship, and the simple things of life, intentionally leaving behind the pressures of our occupations. We come back truly refreshed, ready to give ourselves fully to our callings.

When you take a day off, really take a day off. Turn off your cellphone. The world won't stop turning because you spend the day at the zoo with your kids or your friends. When you go on vacation, leave your laptop and Palm Pilot at home, and don't give in to the temptation to visit an Internet café to check your e-mail. Learn the discipline of rest and recreation.

As you continue planning and working toward your goals, commit everything you do to the Lord. As the writer of Proverbs said, "Commit to the LORD whatever you do, and your plans will succeed."[9]

For Personal Reflection or Group Discussion

1. Using the guidelines discussed in this chapter, define your personal mission statement.

2. Next, define your vision statement. (Remember, your strategies for reaching your purpose will evolve over time.)

3. What are three practical goals that will help propel you toward achieving your vision in the coming year?

Chapter Ten

Dream Thieves

I have spread my dreams under your feet;
Tread softly because you tread on my dreams.

William Butler Yeats,
"He Wishes for the Cloths of Heaven,"
1899

If a robber broke into your home, what would you do? Most likely you would grab the nearest telephone and call the police. You might confront the robber if you had a weapon. Unless he threatened you or your family with violence, you would never allow him to lounge on your sofa, eat your food, watch your television, and play with your children!

Yet when it comes to thieves of the heart, many people unknowingly allow these robbers to make themselves at home in the deepest places of their heart. Rather than viewing them as enemies to evict, they consider them unpleasant facets of their personality. Over time, the dream thieves become integrated into their identity.

Thieves of the heart are exceptionally crafty, sneaking in through the unlocked doors of unhealed emotional wounds, fears, doubts, and unresolved issues from the past. If not identified and captured, dream thieves will steal your vision, rob you of courage, and immobilize you from ever fulfilling your purpose.

Remember this: You are most vulnerable to dream thieves just when you decide to get serious about pursuing your purpose. You've tapped into your heart's desires, prayed for revelation, defined your vision statement, and written out your goals. Enthusiastic and motivated, you are taking practical steps toward achieving those goals.

Thieves of the heart are exceptionally crafty, sneaking in through the unlocked doors of unhealed emotional wounds, fears, doubts, and unresolved issues from the past. If not identified and captured, dream thieves will steal your vision, rob you of courage, and immobilize you from ever fulfilling your purpose.

Suddenly the dream thieves strike with vengeance.

Your commitment to reach for your dreams is often the very trigger that exposes them. Unresolved fears surface, overwhelming you with feelings of intimidation. Self-doubt rears its ugly head. Memories of critical, undermining words spoken to you begin to play over and over in your mind like a broken record.

Never forget, the bigger your dream, the more dream thieves you will encounter. Fear is by far the most common and destructive dream thief and the main reason why many people never reach their purpose. For that reason, I have devoted the entire next chapter to dealing with fear. In this chapter, we will look at other common ways our dreams are sabotaged.

The Mockers

Countless dreams are robbed by insensitive and critical attitudes and words. Give too much heed to other people's opinions and you'll never reach your dreams. Vision will become blurred, motivation will diminish, and eventually you may give up.

Ask yourself these questions: *Is my sense of identity easily shaken by other people's opinions? Am I desperate for approval from others? Do I become confused or double-minded when someone criticizes me? Do I feel emotionally crushed if people don't give me the support and affirmation I desire?*

If you answered yes to one or more of these questions, it's time to deal with the mockers.

Keep in mind that although some people are intentionally critical, many are oblivious to the destructive impact of their negative words.

Regardless of the intent of criticism, we must learn to respond with wisdom and grace. Accept the fact that the world is full of mockers. That's life. If you allow other people's opinions to shake your sense of identity and erode your confidence in your dream, you'll never go very far on the pathway of purpose.

Many people today suffer from the "crab mentality"—a deeply ingrained tendency to pull other people down to their level.

Researchers who were studying the behaviour of crabs placed a hundred or so in a large container to see how they would respond to confinement. Though all the crabs struggled to escape, their success was hindered by what the scientists called "suppression." Just as a crab was about to succeed in getting out of the container, another would use its claws to pull it down.

People with a crab mentality feel threatened when someone attempts to break out of her box and pursue her dream. Misery loves company. A surprising number of people are determined to bring others down to their level. Those stuck in the rut of mediocrity are especially prone to the crab mentality.

When someone decides to step out of her comfort zone and attempt great achievements, the "crabs" feel threatened. People with no vision are confronted with their own shortcomings when encountering someone with a big dream. Observing someone break out of her box reminds them of their own limitations. Often, they respond by criticizing the person who is pursuing a dream.

As Cheryl Richardson says, "When you accomplish great things you tap into the unhealed wounds of those around you and remind them of their own lost dreams or unmet needs."[1]

When we realize that most critical people are simply responding to their own brokenness, we are less likely to be hurt by their arrows.

Katherine found herself surrounded by supportive friends in a time of terrible crisis. Her husband had left her for another woman; one week later she lost her job, and she had three teenaged children to support.

During her darkest days, friends lavished Katherine with support and encouragement. They took her out for lunch, bought her groceries, telephoned her daily, and made themselves available for whatever she needed.

A year later, Katherine was back on her feet emotionally and anticipating a bright future. Thanks to financial help from her brother, she had started a new business. Already it was generating enough revenue to support her family. Having discovered an entrepreneurial gift that she didn't even know she had, Katherine was already planning for expansion.

You would have thought that Katherine's friends would have been thrilled for her. Instead, the large circle of supporting friends dwindled to just two. The others started making nasty comments like "She really thinks she's something, doesn't she?" "She's certainly gotten big for her britches." "Isn't it weird how she goes around looking so happy when her husband left her last year? Maybe he had good reasons for leaving."

Unfortunately, Katherine's experience is not unique. Don't be surprised if you find that people are wonderfully supportive when you are down and struggling but critical or indifferent when you start to succeed. Though people should be motivated and encouraged by someone else's success, in reality many become threatened and insecure. Like the crabs, they will try to pull you down if it looks like you just might make it over the top.

How should we respond to the mockers?

We can take the easy way out and crawl into a safe little cocoon to avoid criticism, but that's not living—it's merely surviving.

Be careful to protect your heart when confronted with mockers. There's a delicate balance. On one hand, we must guard our hearts against inappropriate criticism, refusing to allow other people's poisonous words and attitudes to fester and guarding against anger or bitterness. On the other hand, while guarding our hearts, we must avoid building walls. There is a real difference between boundaries and walls. Wise people establish healthy boundaries; one example of a healthy boundary is refusing to spend much time with critical and negative people.

Just be careful you don't harden your heart in the process. It will hinder your relationship with God and prevent you from experiencing intimate friendships with others.

Keep your heart pure, remembering that most critical people are wounded and insecure individuals. Pray for them and maintain a gracious and forgiving attitude. Be kind to the mockers, but refuse to allow their poisons to penetrate your heart. Avoid playing their comments over and over in your mind, for it will drain your faith and courage.

As you press forward on the pathway of purpose, you will encounter critics from time to time who mock your dreams. Keep your heart right, and God will use the words of the mockers for your good. As you learn to respond graciously to criticism, your faith grows and your character matures.

On several occasions, God used "mockers" to strengthen my faith. At one time, I would dwell on memories of other people's negative and demeaning comments or attitudes. When I did, I became double-minded. My faith wavered. Some days I was full of vision and enthusiasm; other days, when I dwelt on the words of the mockers, I became discouraged and unmotivated.

My biggest problem was not the critics. My problem was my response. By dwelling on their negative words and attitudes, I was internalizing their criticism. It drained my faith and motivation.

As I developed the habit of bringing criticism to God in prayer, I received wisdom for objectively weighing other people's comments and the ability to evaluate if there was any truth in them. Sometimes, pebbles of truth can be discovered in a mountain of inappropriate criticism. If I discern any truths in the criticism, I take them to heart, but I am careful to discard everything else.

Pray for wisdom to distinguish between constructive and destructive criticism. Ask God for the humility to receive truth and the grace to let go of everything else.

Another valuable tool for guarding your heart from the critics is to cultivate friendships with spiritually mature, wise individuals who are also visionaries committed to walking by faith.

It would be wonderful if everyone were supportive and encouraging, affirming your dreams and saying, "Go for it! I believe in you!" In reality, there may be just a handful who will stand with you, and perhaps only one or two. This is especially true in the beginning, when you have a dream but no visible outward success.

I have learned to keep my dreams close to my heart in the initial stages, sharing them only with my husband and a few trusted friends. Dreams should be treated like a baby growing in her mother's womb. In the first months of gestation, the baby is most vulnerable; this is the time when miscarriages are most likely to occur.

When your dream is in its initial formative stages, gestating in the womb of your heart, avoid sharing it prematurely. It is imperative to seek wise counsel, of course. But use discretion. Pray and ask God to lead you to those with spiritual maturity and wisdom.

Sometimes, pebbles of truth can be discovered in a mountain of inappropriate criticism. If I discern any truths in the criticism, I take them to heart, but I am careful to discard everything else.

And don't rush the process. God may want you to nurture your dreams in the womb of your spirit for a season, to bathe them in prayer before you share them with others.

When you do share your dreams with trusted friends, maintain a humble heart. A God-inspired dream can stand up to questions and challenges. Don't be threatened by questions from those who truly care about you. God may use others to provide insight and wisdom, to reveal adjustments that need to be made or problems that need to be addressed.

At times, God may use your family or friends to show you that you are on the wrong track. For example, perhaps you are pursuing a dream out of insecurity. If so, this needs to be exposed so you can deal with the insecurities that are pushing you in a direction that is not God's plan for you.

The Inner Critics

Though the "crabs" will snatch your dreams if you let them, you're far more likely to be robbed by inner critics.

I read a newspaper article about four thieves who stole $100 million worth of diamonds from the world's largest diamond centre in Antwerp, Belgium. What was truly amazing about this theft was that this particular diamond centre had one of the most expensive security systems in the world. Despite round-the-clock police presence, state-of-the-art security cameras, and a complex system of secret codes, the robbers emptied two-thirds of the building's maximum-security vaults and walked away without an alarm being raised or a shot being fired. Though the robbers were arrested a week later, their success in avoiding detection by the state-of-the-art security equipment baffled police and security experts.

In the same way, inner dream thieves are exceptionally crafty. Skulking through the vulnerable corridors of our hearts, they erode confidence in our dreams. Yet many people have no idea how or when these precious treasures were stolen. In many cases, inner dream thieves work undetected for so many years that people view them as a part of their identity rather than as enemies that must be evicted.

The tragic result is that we become our own worst enemies. Many of us start beating ourselves up early in life. As adults, the voices of inner critics become loudest, harshest, and most demanding of our attention just when we give ourselves permission to explore the desires of our hearts. (I'm not talking about actual voices, of course, but rather, inner thoughts and emotions.)

For example, when I began writing my first book, I was taunted by inner thoughts like, *Who do you think you are? You can't write a book. You don't have anything of value to say. Nobody will want to read it.*

If you dare to step out of your comfort zone, be prepared to confront inner dream thieves in the form of thoughts like, *Who do you think you are? You can't do this. People will laugh at you when you fail. This is too big for you—you'll never succeed.*

Self-condemnation may also rear its ugly head, reminding you, *Remember what you did—remember how you failed that time? You'll fail again. You don't deserve to succeed.*

Inferiority may taunt, *God can use other people, but not you. You have no talents. You're too timid. You're flawed.*

Unchecked, these inner voices will steal your dreams.

If inner dream thieves have robbed you, don't wait another day to confront them. The first step is to acknowledge them. If you try to bury your doubts and insecurities, they won't remain hidden for long. Time and again they will push their way into your consciousness, erupting in your thoughts and emotions, swaying your choices and actions, and ultimately thwarting your destiny.

If not captured, inner dream thieves will continually draw attention to your blemishes and imperfections, your scars and handicaps, and your inadequacies and shortcomings—instead of your potential and possibilities in God. These voices must be dealt a fatal blow or they will rob your faith and courage, immobilizing you from going forward.

I'm sure you have discovered that negative thoughts will war against your faith. When those thoughts come, refuse to dwell on them. Otherwise, they will penetrate your heart, erode your confidence, and eventually snuff out your dreams.

Replace the lies of the inner critics with the truths in God's Word. As light dispels darkness, the truth of God's Word will uproot and dispel lies in your soul, and as Jesus said, "Then you will know the truth, and the truth will set you free."[2]

If you struggle with feelings of inferiority, study Bible verses that describe God's love for you. If you are afraid of failure, study Scriptures that affirm how God wants to bless and prosper you. Reflect on these truths until you truly believe them in your heart.[*]

Each time negative thoughts surface, focus on what God says about you rather than the lies of the inner critics. This will take time, especially if you have been in the habit of dwelling on negative thoughts about yourself.

Pray out loud, thanking God for what his Word says about you. If the inner critics are saying, *You can never accomplish anything; you'll never reach your dream*, pray, *God, I thank you that though I can do nothing of value on my own, my dependence is upon you, and "I can do everything through him who gives me strength."*[3]

If the inner critics are telling you that you're a failure, that God is displeased with you, pray, *God, I thank you that you love me with an everlasting love, and nothing I can do or not do will change that. I thank you that you have recreated me as the righteousness of God in Christ Jesus. I am righteous because of you, not me.*[4]

We all have shattered hopes and dreams—memories of times when we thought God was leading us a certain way, and it didn't work out.

---

[*] Bible verses about God's love: Jeremiah 31:3; John 3:16; Ephesians 3:17–19; 1 John 3:1

You may have stepped out in faith and—boom! Everything disintegrated into ashes of failure.

Focusing on failures will paralyze you, keeping you from ever risking or dreaming again. When those memories surface, pray, *God, I thank you that I am your child and your Holy Spirit has been teaching me to hear your voice more clearly and know you more intimately. I thank you that you have forgiven me. Thank you for your promise to instruct me and teach me in the way I should go.*[5]

Never allow failure to immobilize you. Don't beat yourself up over the times you have incorrectly interpreted God's leading. I don't know anyone who hasn't made mistakes in this area. See failure as an opportunity to learn and grow. You are only a failure if you never try or if you give up after making a mistake.

The late Jamie Buckingham wrote, "The risk-free life is a victory-free life. It means lifelong surrender to the mediocre. And that is the worst of all defeats."

Other inner dream thieves can be real or imagined limitations, such as a lack of skills, training, time, talents, and so forth. We all face limitations. But the Bible promises that God's strength is perfected in weakness. Nothing can limit God. If he has given you a dream, he will empower you to fulfill it.

Character Compromise

Compromising biblical standards is perhaps the most subtle of the dream thieves, making it especially dangerous.

One morning, while I was working feverishly to meet a project deadline, a friend telephoned. "Do you have time to talk?" she asked. My response was curt, "Well, I have a couple of minutes. I'm on deadline, and I really don't have time during office hours for personal calls. Can I call you this evening instead?" Her voice shook as she quietly replied, "Oh, sorry, sure, I'll call you tonight."

Alarm bells went off in my heart. I asked, "What's wrong?" After a few seconds of silence, she said, "Gary [her husband] just left. He's found another woman."

Oh, did I feel small. This was not the first time I had responded impatiently when someone interrupted my well-planned schedule.

143

Before this incident, I justified my actions. After all, I didn't like interruptions because I was committed to focusing on the goals God had given me. (Now, wasn't that spiritual of me?)

Never allow failure to immobilize you. Don't beat yourself up over the times you have incorrectly interpreted God's leading. I don't know anyone who hasn't made mistakes in this area. See failure as an opportunity to learn and grow. You are only a failure if you never try or if you give up after making a mistake.

This is an example of trying to make the end justify the means. My "end" in this case was accomplishing a worthwhile goal. My "means" was compromising on biblical values (kindness, selfless love) to reach this goal.

Any way you look at it, it was sin. I have learned that God is far more concerned about my character than my achievements.

Integrity in financial affairs is a common area of compromise. I know business owners who believe that because they financially support missions or other ministries, they are justified in cheating on their income tax, mistreating employees, or getting involved in shady business deals. After all, isn't some of their money going to good causes?

To truly walk in the fullness of purpose, we must not only do God's will, we must do it God's way—with integrity and unwavering adherence to biblical truth.

As the Lord says, "As the heavens are higher than the earth, so are my ways higher than your ways and my thoughts than your thoughts."[6]

Take shortcuts to fulfilling your dreams, and I guarantee you'll be buffeted by one setback after another.

Compromise is deceptive, for it often involves partial obedience. It is more dangerous than outright rebellion, for its very subtlety makes it easy to deny or justify.

Compromise will rob you in many ways, the greatest price being intimacy with God. The Psalmist wrote, "The secret [of the sweet, satisfying companionship] of the Lord have they who fear (revere and worship) Him, and He will show them His covenant and reveal to them its [deep, inner] meaning."[7]

Another price of compromise is losing out on the many blessings God desires for us. In Deuteronomy Chapter 28, the Bible provides dozens of promises of the abundant blessings that God wants to pour out on our lives—personally, relationally, spiritually, financially, and in our occupations and ministries. But there is a condition to these blessings: fully obeying God and his Word.[8]

Prior to Joshua's leading the Israelites into the Promised Land of Canaan, God warned, "Be careful to obey all the law . . . do not turn from it to the right or to the left, that you may be successful wherever you go."[9]

When they followed these instructions, they succeeded. When they compromised, they failed miserably.

Remember when the army of Israel experienced spectacular victory in conquering the first city, Jericho? Excited and confident, they went on to their next target, the city of Ai. No doubt they had a sense of invincibility as they approached the city, still heady from their triumph at Jericho.

Instead of the anticipated victory, they were utterly defeated and humiliated. Joshua, their leader, was stunned. His first reaction was to blame God. "God, why did you do this to me? You told us to conquer this city, and then you let us down—you let us get totally defeated by our enemies. I look like a fool. You told me to take this city and stood by and did nothing while we experienced humiliating defeat. What am I going to tell everyone? What are people going to think?" (my paraphrase of Joshua 7:7–9).

Joshua's next statement was the icing on the cake. "What then will you do for your own great name?"[10] Or, in contemporary language, "Lord, look how bad our defeat makes *you* look!"

God was not impressed with Joshua's pity party. He said, "Stand up! What are you doing down on your face? Israel has sinned; they have violated my covenant, which I commanded them to keep. . . . That is why the Israelites cannot stand against their enemies."[11]

Have you ever blamed God when things turned out wrong? I have. Oh, not with my words or even with conscious thoughts, but my heart attitude blamed him. Deep down, I felt as though God had let me down.

Later, I often realized I had compromised in some way. At times,

I had succumbed to pride or other sinful attitudes. Other times, I had only partially obeyed God.

Israel's defeat had absolutely nothing to do with the strength, intelligence, or weaponry of the people of Ai. God did not let them down. Their problem was sin. Sin removed God's protection and left them vulnerable.

Sin in our lives also removes God's protection and leaves us vulnerable to satanic attack.

I am *not* implying that satanic opposition is always the result of sin. To the contrary, the more we step out in faith, the more intense and relentless the spiritual opposition. Those who are pursuing a God-inspired dream will encounter far more satanic opposition than those who live in mediocrity.

Satanic attack does not mean you are compromising on biblical principles. However, if you find yourself consistently defeated in a particular area, it's possible that compromise is a contributing factor. Ask the Holy Spirit to search your heart and see if you have opened a door to Satan through compromise.

If God illuminates an area of compromise, repent. Then move on. Avoid wallowing in self-condemnation and press forward on your journey of faith.

Mediocrity

Mediocrity robs many people of their dreams. *Merriam-Webster* defines *mediocre*: "of moderate or low quality, value, ability, or performance." The *Collins* dictionary uses this definition: "neither bad nor good, ordinary, middling, second-rate."

My father frequently hired mentally disabled persons to work in the souvenir-production division of his business. I was amazed by how energetically and joyfully they worked. They were especially proud to receive a paycheque for their work.

Joey, who had Down syndrome, was one of those workers. He would rise before dawn to pack his lunch, eager for morning to arrive so he could board the bus that transported him to his job at Dad's business. From 8 a.m. until 5 p.m., Joey applied decals to souvenir collector spoons.

Much like an artist applying brush to canvas, Joey would peel a self-sticking decal from its wrapper, painstakingly centre it over the base of the spoon, and slowly press it on the metal. If the decal was not perfectly centred, he peeled it off and started over. He glowed with pride over the racks of completed spoons ready to be packaged for shipping to stores.

Joey exemplified unwavering commitment to excellence, doing his very best with his abilities and resources. He refused to allow one iota of mediocrity to infiltrate his attitudes or his work.

Joey will never become the chairman of a Fortune 500 company, and it's unlikely he will ever win an Academy Award or a Pulitzer Prize, but though he may never achieve great success according to the standards of this world, in God's eyes he is an outstanding success, a source of continual pride and joy to his heavenly Father.

To reach our dreams, we must embrace excellence and shun mediocrity, guarding against its intrusion into our attitudes and endeavours.

Without a passionate commitment to pursue your dream, it is all too easy to settle for second best or to compromise your ideals to make them more acceptable to the mediocrity crowd.

The Bible says, "The people who know their God shall prove themselves strong and shall stand firm and do exploits."[12]

Great exploits are not measured by fame or by the accolades of others. Nor are they measured by the visible magnitude of their impact. They are measured by doing our very best with what God has given us.

Are you a mother with small children? What is your vision for parenting? You can be a nice, sweet parent who raises nice, well-behaved children who do well in school and go to college and excel in their career and marry someone nice with a good job. Of course, that is all very nice.

Or—you can be a Spirit-empowered, visionary parent who raises world changers who alter the course of history.

This exemplifies the difference between mediocrity and excellence—between doing good things and accomplishing great exploits.

Mediocrity is a stench to God. It is an affront to all that he is and does and desires to do in and through our lives.

As God's image-bearers, let's despise mediocrity. Let's seek to be more passionate, creative, and excellent in everything we do. Let's refuse the well-travelled path of mediocrity, predictability, and conformity, instead choosing the less-travelled path of faith, courage, and excellence.

As you can see, dream thieves come in many shapes and disguises. Learn to recognize the varied ways in which dream thieves will try to rob your purpose, and deal with them immediately and aggressively.

Always remember, the bigger your dream, the more dream thieves you will encounter. Be vigilant to guard the precious treasures of purpose that God has entrusted to you.

When you know you have a divinely inspired dream, never let go. Refuse to swim in waters of mediocrity, where the "crabs" like to hang out. I realize it is much easier to swim in those calm waters. There is no resistance. You can just float along with the tide. Great crowds of people swim there, and you will find a lot of acceptance and very little opposition.

Choose to swim instead in the great tides of purpose. It won't be easy. You'll be lonely, for not many swim in these isolated waters. It will be hard, for you will often feel as though you are swimming against the tide. At times, it will seem as though the waves will be too great and powerful for you to overcome. Fatigue will overwhelm you. You'll be tempted to quit. Every day you will hear the mediocre mockers trying to convince you to join them in their quiet, undisturbed ponds.

But lift your head above the waves and look to the horizon. It is painted with glorious colours of purpose and destiny. It is yours. Keep swimming.

For Personal Reflection or Group Discussion

1. Is there a "dream thief" that you have believed was part of your identity rather than something God wants to free you from? How has it affected you?

2. Have other people's opinions or criticism held you back from pursuing your goals? How?

3. We all face inner critics from time to time. How do you deal with self-condemning thoughts and feelings?

4. Do you strive for excellence? If not, what is one step you will take to change this?

Chapter Eleven

Conquering Fear

Always do what you are afraid to do.

Ralph Waldo Emerson,
"Heroism," *Essays: First Series*

I cringed lower into the seat of my grey metal desk, yearning for the faded yellow floor to swallow me into oblivion. A crimson heat spread from my forehead to my neck; my legs trembled uncontrollably. I struggled to bring my lurching stomach under control—vomiting all over my classmates was about the only thing that could worsen this nightmare.

My panic attack was provoked by my fifth-grade teacher's request that I come to the front of the class and recite a few lines from Emily Dickinson's poem, "A Slash of Blue."

I knew the verses. That wasn't my problem. The night before, I had recited the poem to my three-year-old sister, Dianne. But an adoring baby sister was one thing—a classroom full of peers was another matter entirely.

I finally dragged myself to the front of the class. Trembling from head to foot, my face burning with humiliation, I somehow managed to avoid crying as I choked out each word. It was several hours before the trembling stopped.

My terror of public speaking worsened over the years, driving me to Herculean efforts to avoid situations that posed a remote risk of having to say a few words to a group. In high school, I avoided participating in class discussions. At university, I refused to sign up for courses that required oral presentations.

You can imagine my dismay years later when God spoke to my heart during prayer that part of his purpose for me was speaking. *Me?* I gasped. *Lord, you must be kidding. Please, not that. Anything but speaking!*

Despite the terror provoked by this idea, something resonated in my spirit—something so deep it was barely discernible. It was as though a hidden jewel of purpose was being unearthed from its long-hidden burial place. I comforted myself with thoughts that if God really was leading me to do some public speaking, it would probably happen ten or twenty years in the future, after he had set me free from those fears.

Just three weeks later, I was astonished to receive an invitation to speak at a ladies' conference. The coordinator of the function said she expected about three hundred ladies. Though everything inside of me squirmed with intimidation, though my mind screamed at me to say no, I knew God wanted me to accept the invitation.

Anxiety plagued me from the moment I accepted the invitation until the conference eight weeks later. I couldn't sleep. I lost weight. As the event drew nearer, I entertained fantasies of natural disasters forcing a cancellation, like the worst blizzard in Canadian history striking the city.

Alas, the dreaded night arrived. During the preliminaries, I was glued to my seat, frozen in fear. My heart pounded so loud I was sure everyone could hear it. My legs vibrated like the unbalanced wheels in my old Toyota; I was relieved that I had worn a long skirt.

Finally, I was introduced. The walk to the front of the room seemed to take forever. When I stood before the podium, I trembled so violently that I had to use both hands to hold the microphone. I peeked out at a very intimidating audience and opened my mouth. Faint with fear, my facial muscles twitching uncontrollably, I somehow stumbled through my introduction.

About one minute later, an amazing miracle occurred—my entire being was flooded with a river of peace, flushing away the fear and filling me with an overwhelming sense of God's presence. Boldness and authority displaced my fear and intimidation, and the rest of my message flowed easily.

Needless to say, this instant and dramatic release from fear spurred my faith to a whole new level, giving me just enough courage to say yes the next time I was invited to speak. Even so, I continued to suffer through weeks of anxiety prior to any speaking engagements over the next couple of years. But each time, the anxiety lessened. Each time, it became a little easier.

As I continued to step out in faith despite my fears, the time finally came when I was completely free of my terror of public speaking.

What if I had never faced this fear? What if I had remained huddled in a safe cocoon, refusing to step out of my comfort zone? I have no doubt that my life would be very different today, for I have discovered that conquering fear in one area results in breakthroughs over fear in other areas as well.

Some of my greatest personal breakthroughs have come as I stepped out and obeyed God despite overwhelming fear.

"You gain strength, courage, and confidence by every experience in which you really stop to look fear in the face," said Eleanor Roosevelt. "You must do the things you think you cannot do."

Fear: A Robber

What gifts are buried beneath your fears? What passions have been quenched by intimidation? What dreams have been forfeited in exchange for the shallow security of avoiding the things that make you uncomfortable?

To conquer fear, you must be willing to admit the consequences of remaining its prisoner. Following are the major repercussions of succumbing to fear.

Undiscerned Potential

Some gifts, abilities, and divinely inspired passions are easy to discern. Others may be hidden beneath shrouds of fear. That was the case for me in the area of public speaking.

Have you ever said or thought these words, *That's just not me?* How can you be sure, if you haven't conquered fear in your life? If you view yourself through the lens of intimidation, you may be blinded to treasures God has placed in you.

Recently, I went hiking with my husband in the Radium Hot Springs area of British Columbia. The trail started at the creek bed of the Sinclair Canyon, then wound up and up and up. We were amazed at how different the mountains, valleys, and canyon looked from different vantage points on the trail. When we were at Sinclair Creek at the bottom of the canyon, the chasm walls were huge and overpowering. At the top of the trail, the same rock walls looked small and insignificant. From that high vantage point, we could see hundreds of mountain peaks in the Sinclair and Rocky Mountain ranges that were hidden from view at the base of the Sinclair Canyon.

Canyons of fear will blind you to your potential. If you will commit to conquering intimidation, God will lift you to a high vantage point of faith, where your spiritual vision will be enlightened to see vast new horizons of beauty and potential.

Dormant Gifts

The apostle Paul wrote to Timothy, "Do not neglect your gift, which was given you through a prophetic message when the body of elders laid their hands on you."[1]

Why was Timothy neglecting his gifts? Clues are revealed in another letter Paul wrote to Timothy two years later.

> For this reason I remind you to fan into flame the gift of God, which is in you through the laying on of my hands. For God did not give us a spirit of timidity, but a spirit of power, of love and of self-discipline.[2]

A "spirit of timidity" had been holding Timothy back from using his gifts. *Timidity* is the root of the word *intimidation*. Paul exhorted Timothy to trust in God's power and love rather than succumb to fear and intimidation.

Surrender to fear and you will neglect your gifts. Fear will not only rob you of the joy of fulfilling your purpose, it will also rob many other people of the blessings God wants to release through your gifts and talents.

Slavery to Other People's Opinions

Another price of fear is becoming a slave to other people's opinions, trapped by thoughts such as, *If I try something new, will I look like a fool? What if I fail? What will people think? If I tell people my dreams, will they laugh at me? Will they mock me?*

Fear of rejection or criticism will keep you from pursuing your goals and dreams. You'll become confused, assailed by self-doubt when others criticize you or don't encourage you.

It's all too easy to become distracted by the opinions of others, wasting emotional energy worrying about what other people think about you. Remember the proverb that says the "fear of man will prove to be a snare," but "the fear of the LORD is a fountain of life."[3]

The "fear of man" refers to being more concerned about pleasing people than pleasing God. Desiring other people's approval more than God's will hinder us from embracing our calling.

Self-destructive Choices

Fear is at the root of many self-destructive choices. Some people marry the wrong person because they fear being alone. Others, fearing intimacy, keep everyone at a distance. Still others succumb to one dysfunctional or abusive relationship after another. Some married couples settle for superficiality in their relationship because fear of confrontation keeps them from discussing difficult issues.

Many people work at jobs they hate for fear of not having financial security. Some never step out of their comfort zone to try something new, fearing the unknown. Many settle for mediocrity, for they fear the risk of failure.

Missed Blessings

The Bible tells the story of Joshua and the Israelites taking possession of the Promised Land, Canaan. Canaan is symbolic of all the promises in God's Word and all the promises that the Holy Spirit has quickened to you personally. The apostle Paul says, "For no matter how many promises God has made, they are 'Yes' in Christ."[4]

I'm sure you have discovered that the promises in God's Word are not just dropped into our laps. We must possess them by faith.

Though Joshua and that generation of Israelites did indeed possess most of Canaan by faith, we know that most of the previous generation did not. They had the same opportunities and the same God working on their behalf, but they never entered the Promised Land. Why? Because of fear and unbelief.

Fear will keep you from ever possessing your own Canaan. It will hinder you from receiving all the blessings that God desires to pour into your life.

Limited Character Growth

Huddling in a safe cocoon may protect you from facing the things you fear, but you will also be bored (many people repress their boredom by distracting themselves with material possessions and meaningless activities). You'll be easily intimidated. Your character will remain weak—for overcoming fear is one of the ways that character is strengthened. Most importantly, you will never embrace the purpose God has for you.

Remember this: You could very well tap into the greatest anointing of the Holy Spirit in the same areas in which you are now battling the most debilitating fears. Satan will attack you most in areas where you have the most potential to glorify God. Conquering fear requires total dependence on God. The more you rely on the Holy Spirit, the greater will be the anointing you receive for service.

Love: The Foundation of Courage

Courage is built upon the foundation of God's love. The Bible says, "God is love. . . . There is no fear in love. But perfect love drives out fear."[5]

Some fears are the natural result of stepping out in faith; these are conquered by facing the things you fear. Other fears are rooted in identity issues, especially inferiority. When you feel inferior, it's hard to believe God is faithful. It's difficult to believe he truly loves you and desires to bless you. Living by faith is tough when you have a warped perception of God's character.

There's only one solution to inferiority—and it's not going through years of therapy and self-contemplation in an attempt to analyze all the reasons *why* you struggle with inferiority. The solution is to become secure in God's love for you. This applies regardless of what life experiences may have contributed to the inferiorities.

Early in my Christian walk, the Holy Spirit revealed to me that I had a root of inferiority. Previously, I had denied those feelings, even to myself, and wore an outward mask of confidence and invincibility. In prayer, God showed me how inferiority was limiting me. He directed me to get out my Bible and underline all the Scriptures about God's love and faithfulness, then meditate on these truths every day, taking time to really ponder them in my heart.

Remember this: You could very well tap into the greatest anointing of the Holy Spirit in the same areas in which you are now battling the most debilitating fears. Satan will attack you most in areas where you have the most potential to glorify God.

For the first few weeks, there were no discernible changes, but after a couple of months I noticed that the feelings of inferiority had diminished. After about six months, inferiority was completely destroyed. It was an amazing miracle—one I shall never forget.

As I meditated on God's Word, truth penetrated the lies embedded in my soul, releasing me to receive a wonderful, liberating revelation of God's love for me. Secure in God's love, I experienced unshakeable strength and confidence. I no longer had to wear a mask.

Trust grows to the degree that we have a revelation of the goodness, love, and faithfulness of our heavenly Father. God's love is far greater and more beautiful than anything we could ever comprehend with our physical senses. This is why the apostle Paul prayed that believers would have a "spirit of revelation"—so we can more deeply understand God's love for us. He prayed:

That you, being rooted and established in love, may have power . . . to grasp how wide and long and high and deep is the love of Christ, and to know this love that surpasses knowledge—that you may be filled to the measure of all the fullness of God.[6]

Notice that this love "surpasses knowledge." God's love is far too great to be grasped intellectually. It can only be comprehended spiritually. As we embrace this revelation, we are transformed from the inside out.

This passage of Scripture also reveals that being rooted in God's love is a prerequisite to being filled with his fullness. In other words, we have faith to believe and receive of God's manifold spiritual blessings—including grace, wisdom, revelation, and power (or anointing) for service—as we are more deeply rooted in his love.

For these reasons, it is imperative that you take time every day to experience intimate communion with your heavenly Father. As you consistently spend time in his presence, the light of God's love and truth will dispel the darkness of fear and inferiority.

Pray that the Holy Spirit will give you a revelation of God's love for you. Continually bathe yourself in the love of God. There are many ways of doing this. Listen to worship songs that speak of his love, allowing the lyrics to penetrate deep into your spirit. Meditate on Scriptures that speak of God's love for you. Spend time every day communing quietly in his presence.

I encourage you to be transparent in the presence of your heavenly Father. Open up the closets of your heart and allow him to heal insecurities, build courage, dispel fears, and deepen your revelation of his loving Father's heart. As you grow in understanding God's love for you, inferiority will diminish. Faith and courage will grow, and you will be empowered to face and conquer your fears.

Remember, becoming rooted in God's love is a process. A seed doesn't mature into an oak tree overnight. Moreover, if that seed never receives more than one rain shower a year or one day of sunlight a year, it will never grow much. Growing in God's love is a process. If you commit to spending time each day in his presence, the sunshine of his love, the water of his Spirit, and the nutrients in his Word will build courage, strength, and confidence.

Facing Your Fears

Though gaining a revelation of God's love is foundational to freedom from fear, total victory comes only when you face the things you dread.

The Bible says, "Faith by itself, if it is not accompanied by action, is dead."[7] The Amplified Bible translation says, "So also faith, if it does not have works (deeds and actions of obedience to back it up), by itself is destitute of power (inoperative, dead)."

If you wait until all the anxious feelings are gone before you act in faith, you'll wait forever.

Run from your fears and eventually they will rule you. Each time you surrender to fear, it gains another foothold and occupies more territory. The longer you wait to deal with it, the more areas of your life it will invade.

There is only one way to face fear—head on. When you confront your fears, you will be amazed by the confidence, liberty, and strength that result.

It may help you to realize that fear can be used to your advantage. When you take steps to overcome fear, you must depend on God like never before, and that is the best thing that could ever happen to you. You must also draw from inner reserves. You'll be surprised to discover the vast storehouse of strength God has deposited in you. Jesus' promise is, "My grace is sufficient for you, for my power is made perfect in weakness."[8]

Each time you conquer one fear, you become stronger, and new doors of opportunity open before you. Every step moves you closer to the person you were destined to become, releasing you into greater measures of your purpose.

I was surprised to learn the Bible has 366 verses that warn against fear. In fact, *Fear not* or similar phrases, such as *Be anxious for nothing* or *Be not afraid*, are the most common commands in the Bible. There are more verses telling us not to fear than commands to love, forgive, or be holy.

Fear is by far the biggest obstacle to trusting and obeying God. It is also the number one hindrance to reaching our dreams.

What exactly does *fear not* mean? It is important to understand that *feelings* of fear are not sin—in fact, those feelings are the natural result of "stepping out of the boat" and living by faith. Fear becomes sin when we allow those feelings to dictate our choices and actions (or lack of action). That's when fear robs us of God's purpose and provision.

To some degree, fear will always be with us. Why? Every time we step out in faith to obey God despite feelings of intimidation, we grow. Our faith grows. Our character grows. God opens new opportunities, because he is able to entrust us with greater responsibilities. With each new venture, a new threshold of intimidation must be crossed. So, to some degree, *feelings* of fear will always be the price of living with purpose.

Fear is rarely conquered through a single event or experience; it is conquered progressively as we face our fears one day at a time.

We can never conquer fear in our own strength. Success requires clothing ourselves in the power of God. Before you attempt to face a fear, first build yourself up spiritually through prayer and the Word of God.

The apostle Paul encourages us to "Be strong in the Lord and in his mighty power. Put on the full armor of God so that you can take your stand against the devil's schemes." This passage of Scripture goes on to describe this armour in detail, including prayer, faith, and the Word of God.[9]

After donning this powerful spiritual armour, you must do something with it. You must go into the battlefield. In practical terms, that means facing your fears in everyday life.

Just before Joshua entered the Promised Land, God warned him three different times to not fear. One of the first major hurdles Joshua faced was the Jordan River, which separated the Israelites from the Promised Land. This was no small feat. It was flood season, and the Jordan was literally overflowing its banks. There were no natural means for crossing the Jordan—no bridges, airplanes, or boats. If they tried to swim, they would most certainly drown.

What was Joshua to do? How would they overcome this formidable barrier?

God provided a solution, but it wasn't an easy one. It required a step of faith that involved risking their very lives. God instructed

Joshua to tell the priests to carry the Ark of the Covenant and step right into the raging, flooding Jordan River.[10] Once they stepped into the water, God promised that he would supernaturally part the waters so that all the people could cross. In other words, the miracle would happen *after* they stepped into the raging floodwaters.

Think of the Jordan River as symbolic of obstacles in your life— the inner handicaps or outward circumstances that you consider barriers to reaching your dreams and fulfilling your purpose.

Human nature wants to see the miracle before acting. Human nature says, "Lord, we'll wait on the banks of the Jordan until you part the waters. Once you part the waters, then we'll step into the river."

In practical terms, I could have said, "Lord, I'll wait until you take away my terror of speaking in public, then I'll start using my gifts."

If you wait for a miracle before you take a step of faith, you will never see the miracle. If you wait for God's provision before you give, you will never see his supply. If you wait for all feelings of fear and intimidation to go away before you take risks, those feelings will never go away, and you will never reach your dreams.

Someone once said, "God is the fastest chess player in the world—it's always your move." You move; he moves. If you won't move, neither will he. Why? Three times in the New Testament, it says the righteous will live by faith.[11] Faith is not a feeling; it is expressed as an action of obedience to God, despite feelings or obstacles.

Remember, courage is not the absence of feelings of fear. Courage is boldly stepping out in faith and obeying God despite your feelings of fear, being undaunted by obstacles.

"Courage, of course, like risk, is absolutely relative," writes Gregg Levoy.

> What is courageous to one person may be fainthearted to another. Risk is whatever scares you. It is the threshold we are required to cross before we can lean down to our passions lying dormant and kiss them awake.[12]

Joshua's lessons in courage didn't end with crossing the Jordan River. Possessing the Promised Land required daily steps of courage and obedience. Cities were conquered one at a time. After Joshua and the children of Israel conquered Jericho, they celebrated, taking time to praise God for his faithfulness and rejoice in the victory. But Jericho represented only one small piece of the land God promised them. After Jericho, it was time to take another city. Then another . . . and another.

If you wait for a miracle before you take a step of faith, you will never see the miracle. If you wait for God's provision before you give, you will never see his supply. If you wait for all feelings of fear and intimidation to go away before you take risks, those feelings will never go away, and you will never reach your dreams.

As you commit to take one step despite your fears, then another, fear will lose its grip on your life and you will walk into amazing new thresholds of authority and anointing. You will possess the promises God desires to bring to pass in and through your life.

God set me free from my fear of public speaking. Every time I conquer a new area of fear, I'm challenged to step out of my comfort zone into other endeavours, which inevitably stir up new feelings of intimidation. Each time I obey God by faith, I experience greater measures of freedom and anointing.

Writing my first book was another endeavour that stirred up feelings of intimidation. As a magazine journalist, I had several hundred articles published in periodicals, primarily business magazines. I never felt intimidated about my writings being published, thus I was surprised by the magnitude of intimidation that surfaced while writing my first book, *Freedom versus Feminism*.

One reason was that I felt vulnerable—my book included numerous personal anecdotes. When writing articles on business-related topics, you don't have to be transparent about your personal life.

A greater reason for my intimidation was the book's subject matter. I didn't want to write about a controversial topic in my first book, though I knew God was leading me to do that very thing. Pride and fear were at the root of my resistance—I didn't want anyone to criticize me, and criticism is a given when writing about anything controversial. I wanted people to like me.

In hindsight, I can see that what the Bible calls "the fear of man" was a major stronghold in my life. To truly experience all that God had for me in the future, I needed to let go of my unhealthy preoccupation about other people's opinions. As John Witherspoon said, "It is only the fear of God that can deliver us from the fear of man."

Throughout the process of writing that book, I came up against mountains of intimidation. Each time those feelings surfaced, I prayed and asked God to fill me with fresh grace and courage. Each time, he was faithful to answer this prayer. One boulder at a time, the mountain of intimidation slowly disintegrated.

Finally, my book was published. I remember that day well, for I was amazed that I felt so completely free of the intimidation that had plagued me during the months of writing. It was a wonderful victory, and I celebrated! I was so grateful for the work God had done in me!

Just one week later, God challenged me to take another step of faith. As I was praying for wisdom about how to promote my book, I sensed God directing me to send a copy of my book to the six major Christian television programs in Canada. My stomach sank. *TV! Please God, not that! I could never go on television.*

I finally gave in and mailed copies of my books to the hosts of those television programs, comforting myself with the thought that it was highly unlikely they would be interested in a new, unknown author. Surprise! Over the next week and a half, five out of the six program directors requested an interview. No one was interested in a brief interview, either; the hosts all wanted half-hour or full-hour interviews.

Oh, how I squirmed and wrestled with intimidation during those long, sleepless nights before my first interview. Over and over I thought, *What have I gotten myself into?* But there was no turning back. Once again, I had to throw myself on God's mercy in utter dependence. Once again, I could not depend on my own resources, because this was way beyond my comfort zone.

The time came for the first interview. I felt nervous, but to my surprise it was not all that evident when I watched the program later. During the second interview, the nervousness had significantly diminished.

By the time I did the fifth television program (a full-hour interview on one of the most popular national Christian programs), I felt absolutely no nervousness. None! I was amazed by the peace I felt.

As I sat in the studio waiting for the interview to begin, I remember thinking, *I can't believe this. Here I am about to do an interview on a popular national television program, and I feel total peace. God, you are so amazing.*

I experienced complete ease during the interview. I astonished myself by actually enjoying it!

I have discovered time and again that each step of obedience results in greater freedom and courage. As each area of intimidation is conquered, God opens new doors of opportunity.

Today, I rarely concern myself about other people's opinions (except, of course, those whom I trust and to whom I have made myself accountable). It is so liberating to focus on fulfilling my calling without the emotional distraction of worrying about what people might think.

What fear is God asking you to face? What mountain of intimidation stands between you and your dreams?

When you face your fears in God's strength, you will experience his awesome power working on your behalf. Not only will his grace carry you, it will lift you above the mountains of intimidation to experience wonderful new horizons of purpose. You will be set free to become the person you were created to be, liberated to embrace the wonderful destiny that God has for your life.

Building Your Courage Muscles

One of the principles behind weight training is that you must constantly push yourself beyond what is comfortable. There should be some pain and discomfort, or you'll see little progress.

Building courage is much like building body muscle—it requires consistent exercise. That means getting into the daily practice of resisting fear and obeying God by faith.

The more you work at building courage, the easier it becomes to face your fears. Remember, nobody becomes a giant of courage in a day. It is a lifelong process, one that you must commit yourself to on a regular basis.

Look for ways to stretch yourself. Push yourself beyond what is comfortable. Continually challenge yourself to step out of your comfort zone.

God says, "Enlarge the place of your tent, stretch your tent curtains wide, do not hold back; lengthen your cords, strengthen your stakes. For you will spread out to the right and to the left."13

Enlarge, stretch, lengthen—those are actions God asks us to take. These actions imply discomfort. But as we commit ourselves to stepping out of our comfort zones and allowing God to stretch us, he fills us with more of his Spirit and empowers us with greater courage.

Be proactive about looking for practical opportunities to build your courage muscles. Some people want to hear a booming voice from heaven or see writing on a wall before they take action. Remember, one of the most frequent ways that God communicates is through the Bible. You could spend the rest of your life stepping out in faith by taking one Scripture each day and applying it to your life.

For example, Jesus said we are to pray for the sick. Do you have a sick friend, co-worker, or neighbour? You may be thinking, *Oh, but I would feel embarrassed and uncomfortable to ask if I could pray for her.* If you're feeling uncomfortable, that's good. It means you are stretching yourself. Each time you cross a new threshold of intimidation, you cultivate greater courage.

If you have a habit of avoiding intimacy in relationships, set a goal of inviting someone for coffee once a week, and each time, force yourself to share one thing that is personal.

Are you afraid of public speaking? Look for an opportunity to speak for a few minutes about something that you are passionate about.

Take risks. Do something you are afraid to do. Look for opportunities to do things on a regular basis that cause enough discomfort that you need to depend utterly on God and the promises in his Word.

Today, I can say I am truly grateful for having to battle giants of fear and intimidation in my life. Nothing has been more life changing for me than facing and conquering fear. Nothing has taught me more about God's faithfulness, character, and power than my battles with fear.

If you long to experience the joy of soaring on the wings of faith, the incredible excitement of knowing that you are literally in the centre of God's purposes, the amazing touch of his awesome power—give him permission to knock you out of your safe little nest of security and comfort.

Each time you cross one threshold of intimidation, your courage muscles grow, and you are empowered to handle greater faith ventures. Each time you enter uncharted territory, new feelings of intimidation will surface. That's the price of change. That's the price of living by faith, but the rewards are well worth the temporary pain and discomfort.

Decide today that you will never again allow fear to rob you of your dreams. Commit to rooting yourself in the love of God, facing your fears, and building your courage muscles. If you do your part, God will do his. You'll know the joy of living without limits.

For Personal Reflection or Group Discussion

1. What dreams, gifts, or passions have you repressed because of fear?

2. What new ventures (a ministry, occupation, business, etc.) have you not explored because of fear?

3. Have you avoided intimacy in relationships for fear of getting hurt?

4. Have you made any self-destructive choices because of fear?

5. If you were completely free of fear, how would you be different? What would you do? What would you change?

6. What are some practical actions you can take to build your courage muscles?

Chapter Twelve

Run to Win

*Never give in. Never give in. Never, never,
never, never—in nothing, great or small,
large or petty—never give in, except to
convictions of honour and good sense.*

Winston Churchill

A framed print on my office wall portrays purple and white crocuses poking through a mound of crystallized snow. The inscription on the print reads "Never Give Up. Go over, go under, go around, or go through. But never give up."

When I'm feeling overwhelmed by obstacles and discouragement, this print reminds me that if I persevere, I will fulfill my purpose.

Wilma Rudolph, one of the most celebrated female athletes of all time, knew what it meant to persevere through obstacles to reach for a dream. As a baby, Wilma suffered from one illness after another, including mumps, scarlet fever, and double pneumonia. After polio crippled her left leg and foot, the doctor told her mother Wilma would never walk again.

But Wilma's mother never gave up. She and her other children worked with Wilma on physical therapy day after day, week after week, month and after month, year after year.

Finally, by age twelve, Wilma could walk normally, without crutches, braces, or corrective shoes. It was then that she decided to become an athlete. Her impossible dream came true on September 7, 1960, in Rome, when Wilma became the first American woman to win three gold medals in the Olympics. She won the 100-metre dash and the 200-metre dash and ran the anchor on the 400-metre relay team.

Like Wilma, we need perseverance to reach our dreams. We need spiritual backbone, resilience, and determination. We need unwavering faith that never loses sight of the goal. We need to purpose in our hearts that we will push through obstacles, discouragement, and setbacks until we experience victory.

Reaching your purpose is like running a marathon. The race is different for each of us, for it represents our unique destiny.

But though we run different races, the same attributes are required for winning. The Bible says, "Let us lay aside every weight, and the sin which so easily ensnares us, and let us run with endurance the race that is set before us, looking unto Jesus, the author and finisher of our faith."[1]

Run Lightly

I was never much of an athlete growing up. Notoriously clumsy, I was ostracized by the school volleyball, baseball, and basketball teams. Nevertheless, I did excel in one sport—running. Year after year I won top prizes at school track meets. My long legs, small frame, and low body weight gave me a winning advantage over my competitors.

Long-distance runners know that extra pounds, whether in body weight or clothes, impede speed and performance.

Reaching your dreams also requires running "light." As the Scripture above says, "Lay aside every weight, and the sin which so easily ensnares us."[2]

Sin is easy enough to recognize, and we know what to do with it—repent.

Weights, on the other hand, can be deceiving, for they are often obscured by well-intentioned motives. For example, excessive busyness is a common weight that is often rooted in the inability to say no or set boundaries.

Other encumbrances include excessive amounts of time spent on activities such as hobbies, socializing, watching television, or shopping. All these things can be healthy in moderation, but overindulgence and imbalance will keep you from reaching your goals.

At no other time in history have there been as many distractions as today. Technology is a blessing in many ways; however, the endless availability of electronic toys can also devour our time and energy, leaving little for spiritual pursuits.

It all comes down to a choice between the good and the best, the mediocre and the excellent, the mundane and the significant.

An athlete may enjoy indulging in creamy chocolate desserts now and then with no negative consequences, but no athlete who is truly committed to winning an Olympic gold medal will overindulge in desserts. Why? That type of diet will prevent her from functioning at peak performance.

Balance is crucial for distinguishing between the good and the best. We all need hobbies, a social life, and recreation. But anything that eats up an inordinate amount of your time and distracts you from spiritual pursuits will weigh you down and hinder you from running the race of purpose.

Run with Focus

Running a successful race means staying focused on the big picture. Nothing will throw a runner off stride or slow her down more than turning to look at the runner coming behind her or continually glancing at the crowds to see how they are reacting to her performance.

In the race of purpose, distractions will throw you off stride and sometimes steer you in a direction that leads you farther from, rather than closer to, your dream. Comparing yourself with others or seeking their accolades will also hinder you from running with peak effectiveness. I can't say it enough: You will *never* reach your dreams if you obsess about what other people think.

Allowing yourself to become stressed out over minor annoyances and nuisances will distract you from the big picture. Don't sweat the small stuff. Keep your heart free of emotional clutter, your mind focused on positive thoughts, and your spirit continually attuned to God.

To stay focused on the big picture, you will need to periodically refresh yourself in the promises in God's Word. Accept the fact that you will face setbacks and seemingly insurmountable obstacles along the way. If you become preoccupied with the problem rather than the vision, you may be tempted to give up.

I read a story in *Our Daily Bread* about a little boy who found an abandoned eaglet and raised it on his family's farm. When the eagle matured, it wouldn't fly. Desiring to teach it to fly, he tried throwing it into the air. But each time the eagle looked down, immediately it fell to the ground.

Finally, the little boy had an idea. Lifting the eagle's head, he made it catch a glimpse of the bright sun above. That did it! The eagle pushed out its wings. Then, lifting its head with a shriek, it jumped from the boy's hand and began to soar higher and higher until it was lost to sight in the face of the sun.

Like this eagle, we must lift our vision to the greatness and majesty of our Creator. As we focus on God and his promises, we are energized with fresh faith and empowered to soar to new horizons of purpose.

One of the Bible's greatest leaders, Joshua, needed to be reminded of God's promises. Prior to entering the Promised Land, God reminded Joshua, "Your territory will extend from the desert to Lebanon, and from the great river, the Euphrates—all the Hittite country—to the Great Sea on the west."[3]

This wasn't news—Joshua had heard this promise many times in the past, yet it remained unfulfilled. Why did God remind Joshua of this promise? Was Joshua tempted to give up? I wonder if he battled thoughts like, *Well, I guess we misunderstood God's plan. I guess we didn't hear him after all. We may as well give up.*

Sure, the wilderness was behind them, but formidable obstacles stood between them and the Promised Land. First, they would have to cross the flooding Jordan River. Then they would have to battle powerful enemy armies and capture cities before they could enjoy their inheritance.

Joshua must have been facing discouragement, for God not only reminded him of the promise (including the specific details of the geographical boundaries of the land), he also repeatedly exhorted Joshua not to fear or become discouraged but to trust and believe.

We, like Joshua, suffer intense discouragement at times. Weary from the battle, we begin to wonder, *Will the victory ever come? Perhaps I misinterpreted God's leading. Maybe I should just give up. I've being waiting so long for God's promises to come to pass. I've prayed so long and still have not seen the breakthrough. There's just so much opposition and so many barriers to cross. I can't go on any more.*

At times like those, we need our vision lifted heavenward, just as the little boy lifted the eagle's head before it would fly. Read the wonderful promises in the Bible. Get out your journal and review the personal promises God has given you. Then read them again. When David was fatigued and battle-weary, he "encouraged himself in the LORD his God."[4] In the New Testament, Paul told Timothy to wage spiritual warfare "according to the prophecies previously made concerning you."[5]

Get alone with God and encourage yourself in his presence. Refresh yourself in his promises. Refocus on the vision. Thank God for his faithfulness and remind yourself of the Psalmist's words, "Your love, O LORD, reaches to the heavens, your faithfulness to the skies."[6]

Run with Discipline

Athletes have coined the adage "no pain, no gain," for they know that rigorous training is required to succeed.

Olympic-gold winners endure brutal workouts in which they are challenged at every turn and pushed to their limits. They also adhere to strict diets and tightly scheduled routines, since discipline in all areas of life affects athletic performance.

Discipline is the yoke that harnesses your potential, releasing you to become all you were meant to be. Unfortunately, the very word *discipline* evokes negative feelings in many people. The reality is that excellence in anything requires discipline.

Discipline makes the difference between what you desire to be and what you actually become. It makes the difference between what you say you want to do and what you actually accomplish. For example, ninety-seven percent of people who say they plan to write a book never do. Why? Most are unwilling to pay the price of discipline and hard work.

Practically speaking, discipline means setting realistic goals and establishing a detailed course of action to achieve those goals. This takes humility and accountability. Undisciplined people are always ready with excuses for their inaction.

Discipline could be defined as "faithfulness in action." The apostle Paul said, "To this end I labor, struggling with all his energy, which so powerfully works in me."[7]

Paul was utterly dependent on God's power working in and through him, but he also recognized a key principle: Dependence is active, not passive. That is why Paul said he laboured and struggled.

It is only through God's grace and power that we accomplish anything of significance, but we must appropriate this grace and power. For example, you can pray for God's assistance in finding a better job, but you must do your part and send out your résumés and go for job interviews.

Discipline is the tool that equips us to steward the gifts and opportunities that God provides.

On a practical level, discipline requires effective time management. You would benefit greatly by recording how you spend every thirty-minute block of time for the next two weeks. You may be shocked at all the little ways in which you waste time.

If discipline is a problem for you, make yourself accountable to someone you trust. Share your goals with a friend and once a week report on your progress. Invite her to ask probing questions about how you spent your time. Give her permission to challenge you when you make excuses for wasting it.

Beware of the tyranny of the urgent. Busyness can be the enemy of discipline. Many people justify their busyness, wearing it as badge to broadcast to everyone how responsible they are. They can't say no because their self-worth is based on being in demand. The busier they are, the more indispensable they feel. Though they constantly complain about how busy they are, they wouldn't have it any other way, for that's what makes them feel important.

It is all too easy to get bogged down under life's worries and distractions. Periodically ask yourself these questions: *Am I giving my time and energy to the things that matter most? Or am I consistently settling for the mediocre rather than the best?*

I find that the most helpful way to ensure wise stewardship of my time is to spend the first part of each morning with God. As I spend time in his Word and in prayer, he deposits peace and wisdom into my soul, and my day is far more productive. As Scripture reminds us, "Blessed are all who wait for him!"[8]

On a practical level, effective time management requires using some type of planner. Plan your week, plan your days, and hold yourself accountable for how you spend your time. I suggest you take time at least once a week to scrutinize how you managed your time.

For example, if I planned to write two hours a day on weekdays, but on Tuesday I didn't write at all and on Thursday I only wrote one hour, I make notations in my desk planner about how I spent that time. That way, I can evaluate whether or not I made the right decision. There may have been a good reason for not following my plan—perhaps a friend was hurting and needed me to spend time with her. On the other hand, I may have allowed unimportant distractions to cloud my priorities or I may have succumbed to procrastination.

If you let distractions and meaningless clutter devour your time and energy, you will never reach your dreams. You are the only one who can hold yourself accountable for how you spend your time.

Commit yourself to discipline in your personal life—spiritually, physically, and mentally. Commit yourself to discipline in faithfully and diligently pursuing your calling.

Run with Endurance

I love the feeling of having completed a long distance run, but this feeling comes only after a series of events that severely test my endurance.

The first few minutes are easy. After fifteen to twenty minutes, I hit what runners call the "wall." My side hurts. My leg muscles cramp painfully. My lungs ache. I'm burning up. I feel sluggish, heavy, and fatigued. I've lost my motivation to run, and everything inside me screams, *I can't go any further. I quit!*

Having learned through experience that these moments will pass, I push myself to keep going. After a few more minutes of breathlessness, pain, and exhaustion, I'm suddenly infused with a burst of euphoric energy. My mind is alert and focused. Running becomes effortless, and I easily complete the course. Runners call this the "second wind."

There is perhaps no greater factor in long-term success than endurance. Anyone can be enthusiastic and confident when bursting through the starting gate. But what separates the starters from the finishers is how they respond to obstacles and pain.

"Let me tell you the secret that has led me to my goal," said Louis Pasteur, the French chemist who founded modern microbiology and developed the process of pasteurization. "My strength lies solely in my tenacity."

Be tenaciously determined to finish the course. Push yourself to keep going, despite the obstacles. Keep putting one foot in front of the other. Refuse to give in to feelings of fatigue and discouragement.

Never assume that because you have a dream from God that everything will run smoothly. If you expect an easy stroll down the pathway of purpose, you will be blindsided and crushed when you hit the "wall." No wonder the Bible stresses the need to "run with endurance."[9]

I like the way best-selling author H. Jackson Brown, Jr. describes perseverance in *The Complete Life's Little Instruction Book*: "In the confrontation between the stream and the rock, the stream always wins—not through strength but by perseverance."

We all face the temptation to quit. When battle-weary, discouraged, and besieged by self-doubt, we begin to wonder, *Am I really doing God's will? If so, why is it taking so long to see results? What am I doing wrong? Is it really worth the pain?*

As large regions of Europe fell under the advance of the Nazi war machine, Sir Winston Churchill told the British House of Commons: "We will fight on the beaches, we shall fight on the landing grounds, we shall fight in the fields and in the streets, we shall fight in the hills; we shall never surrender."

If it were not for the tenacity of Mr. Churchill and his unrelenting commitment to fight for freedom, you and I would be living in a very different world today. Freedom—and any worthwhile value or pursuit—comes at a price. And a big part of that price is perseverance.

Giving up wasn't an option for Mr. Churchill. It's not an option for you or me, either, if we truly desire to reach our God-inspired dreams.

Some things should never be surrendered. Your dream is one of them.

Those who choose the path of mediocrity may avoid the pain that accompanies the pursuit of a worthy goal. But people who are passionately committed to the pathway of purpose will encounter one obstacle after another. You will battle gnawing self-doubt, intense discouragement, and, at times, bone-wearying frustration.

As Frank A. Clark said, "If you can find a path with no obstacles, it probably doesn't lead anywhere."

Never assume that because you have a dream from God that everything will run smoothly. If you expect an easy stroll down the pathway of purpose, you will be blindsided and crushed when you hit the "wall." No wonder the Bible stresses the need to "run with endurance."[9]

Persevere. Keep putting one foot in front of the other. You'll see your vision come to pass if you refuse to quit. Then, one glorious day in eternity, you will hear your heavenly Father say, "Well done, good and faithful servant."[10]

Successful visionaries learn to persevere through obstacles. Following are some practical tips for building endurance.

First, drink deeply each day from the fountains of God's grace, love, wisdom, and power through prayer and Scripture reading. This will sustain and strengthen you to continue running the race. The Bible admonishes us to "Be filled with the Spirit."[11] Do this consistently and your spiritual tank will never run dry.

Second, *never* make important decisions when you are feeling discouraged. Think back to the last time you were certain about how God was leading you. You may want to retrieve your journal and find the last place where you recorded the direction in which you believed with all your heart God was leading you.

Commit to continue walking in that direction. Refuse to alter your course when besieged with discouragement and doubt. Like the relentless whine of a violent wind, doubts and fears will drown out the gentle whisper of the Holy Spirit. Always remember that intense discouragement can hinder you from discerning God's direction. Many people feel tempted to make changes when they are discouraged. That is *not* the time to change your direction.

Though God sometimes allows obstacles to get our attention and show us we are on the wrong path, he does that only as a last resort. First he tries to get our attention through his Word, through the inner promptings of the Holy Spirit, or through others that he has placed in our lives.

If you truly believe you took a wrong turn, *first* deal with your discouragement before you consider directional changes. You will be hindered from discerning God's wisdom and leading if you are oppressed by a cloud of discouragement. Wait until the discouragement passes; then seek God for guidance.

If you know you are walking on the right path, continue putting one foot in front of the other. Remain faithful and obedient to the best of your ability. Trust in the faithfulness of your heavenly Father. The second wind of the Holy Spirit will come. And when it comes, you will be rejuvenated, strengthened, and empowered to finish the course that God has set before you.

In the New Testament, the writer of Hebrews says,

> We want each of you to show this same diligence to the very end, in order to make your hope sure. We do not want you to become lazy, but to imitate those who through faith and patience inherit what has been promised.[12]

Refuse to throw away your confidence and you will be richly rewarded. Persevere, knowing that when you do the will of God, you will receive all that he has promised you.

Help the Runner Next to You

Successful runners on the pathway of purpose are not merely concerned about reaching their own dreams; they are also committed to helping others reach theirs.

Author, broadcaster, and columnist Michael Coren tells a story in one of his newspaper columns that exemplifies this team spirit. Several mentally challenged children, including a little boy named George, who had Down syndrome, were competing in a Special Olympics race.

But then disaster. George's legs seemed to become tangled and before he knew what was happening he had fallen. He screamed.

It only took a moment for the other seven runners to leave him yards behind, but George's scream was so loud that they, and the crowd, all heard. Then, gradually, all of them stopped running. Instead of continuing on to victory they all turned around and walked back to where their fellow athlete had fallen.

George was crying now, and holding his cut knees close to his chest. The runners knelt down, cuddled him, wiped away the grit and blood from his legs, and picked him up. They put their arms around him and told him it would be okay. Then they linked arms—all eight of them—and walked forward. Together in a line, as one person, they crossed the finish line. . . . The organizers hurriedly got hold of seven extra gold medals.

When I read this story, I thought, *If only we adults were as caring about others as those children.* Many of us are so preoccupied with our own dreams and goals that we are oblivious to the pain and struggles of those around us.

Let's not become so obsessed with reaching our own finish line that we ignore the dreams, hurts, and discouragement of other runners along the way.

It's all too easy to become so fixated on our vision that we don't even notice, let alone care about, the dreams of others. Consider becoming a mentor to someone else. Commit yourself to that person, providing support through prayer, encouragement, and practical skill development.

As Gary Smalley said in his article "I Believe in You" in *Marriage Partnership* magazine, "As the pressures of life intensify, sometimes the difference between going after a dream and remaining passive is having someone say, 'I believe in you.'"

Don't wait for someone to encourage you. Take the first step. Find someone who is pursuing a dream and stand with her, shoulder to shoulder, and say, "I believe in you."

Run with Faith

As you run your race, your faith will be tested by adversity. You may be running along, feeling on top of the world, bursting with energy and zeal, enjoying a wonderful sense of exhilaration—when suddenly the path abruptly changes. It may stop at the bank of a raging river too deep and turbulent to swim. Or it may suddenly veer upward at a forty-five-degree angle across a seemingly insurmountable rock face.

Untested faith is shaken when buffeted by the storms of life. God tests our faith again and again, not because he is trying to make things difficult for us, but to strengthen our faith so we can accomplish even greater things. Obstacles and setbacks expose unbelief and double-mindedness.

I can be running along, feeling as though I am full of faith and confidence. Suddenly I face a major obstacle, and deep-seated doubts surface. I have come to view this as a positive, albeit frustrating, occurrence. Anything that exposes doubt provides an opportunity for me to grow in faith.

As the Bible says,

> Consider it pure joy, my brothers, whenever you face trials of many kinds, because you know that the testing of your faith develops perseverance. Perseverance must finish its work so that you may be mature and complete, not lacking anything.[13]

You may feel inadequate in the light of the greatness of your dream. You have probably heard the saying, "If your vision isn't so big that it is impossible without God, then it's not big enough."

God is unimpressed by small vision and easy plans. Bruce Wilkinson writes in *The Prayer of Jabez*, "When you take little steps, you don't need God."

God wants to engage us in a vision that is far greater than our natural abilities or resources, for he wants to display his supernatural power and grace. Don't be threatened by feelings of inadequacy—allow them to drive you to depend more deeply on God. After all, success is not based on your power or ability but on God working through you.

Many people feel threatened or defensive when unbelief surfaces. Some respond with denial, pushing their doubts below the surface and refusing to acknowledge them. Sooner or later, though, double-mindedness will emerge in their attitudes and actions.

Glossing over double-mindedness won't make it go away. If you are besieged by doubts, don't beat yourself up—history's greatest champions had to learn to conquer unbelief. In some cases, it took many years.

Untested faith is shaken when buffeted by the storms of life. God tests our faith again and again, not because he is trying to make things difficult for us, but to strengthen our faith so we can accomplish even greater things. Obstacles and setbacks expose unbelief and double-mindedness.

Victory over doubt starts by admitting that it exists, then taking responsibility for dealing with it. If we make excuses like "My grandmother was a negative person and I inherited her spirit of doubt" or "The devil is really attacking me," we will never conquer our doubts.

Patterns of unbelief are sometimes rooted in identity issues. It is imperative to seek God's wisdom about any underlying issues that may be contributing to consistent patterns of doubt. For example, perhaps deep down you don't really believe God loves you. If that is the case, it will be difficult for you to believe that he wants to do great things through your life. You must deal with those root issues, or you will battle doubts again and again (see Chapter 5, *The Restored Heart*).

Don't compare yourself with others who seem to have stronger faith than you have. Just commit yourself to growing in this area. It is important to avoid falling into the trap of beating yourself up every time you succumb to doubts. Just get up, dust yourself off, and persist in pressing through to deeper levels of faith. Remember, self-condemnation is one of the main weapons Satan uses to try and immobilize us and keep us from going further on the pathway of purpose.

Faith is not a feeling; nor is it a matter of getting worked up emotionally. Faith is expressed through active dependence on God and obedience to his Word and revealed will—despite contrary circumstances, thoughts, or feelings. Divine faith produces an inner knowing in your spirit that is deeper and far more reliable than anything you perceive with your physical senses.

Faith is inextricably intertwined with humility, for it takes humility to believe what God's Word says about a situation rather than what our physical senses are telling us.

God rejoices when his children respond to him by faith. One of the best ways you can express your love to God is by believing his Word. The opposite is also true—one of the ways we grieve God most is when we don't trust him. The Bible tells us that "without faith it is impossible to please God."[14]

At times, when struggling with doubt, you may need to engage in spiritual warfare. Remember, Satan will work relentlessly to try to steal dreams from your heart. So also your own doubts and fears will war against God's promises.

God has placed the onus upon us to take up the spiritual weapons he has provided and engage in spiritual warfare. One of those weapons is faith, which the Bible describes as a "shield" in our spiritual armour. A shield represents a defensive part of a soldier's armour; its purpose is to protect from the offensive onslaughts of the enemy. We are reminded that faith will "extinguish all the flaming arrows of the evil one."[15]

Another indispensable weapon, closely linked to faith, is praying and declaring the Word of God. The Bible describes Scripture as "the sword of the Spirit."[16]

A sword is an offensive weapon; it is wielded in direct, aggressive confrontation with an enemy for one purpose: to destroy that enemy. Accurately used, it is deadly.

Several years ago, I faced one of the worst battles with discouragement I had ever encountered. I felt overwhelmed by self-doubt, confusion, depression, spiritual oppression, double-mindedness, and fear of failure. Things seemed hopeless. If my emotional despair wasn't enough, I received bad news about a family member; my computer crashed; I missed a project deadline; my husband was sick; my dishwasher broke down; I had PMS; and my hibiscus plant shed all its blooms that morning. Any way I looked at it, as the children's story goes, "it was a terrible, horrible, no-good, very bad day."

I felt so drained and discouraged that it took everything to just breathe the words "Lord, help!"

I expected God to comfort and reassure me and sympathize with my distress. Instead, he spoke clearly in my spirit, "Stand up! Begin to pray and authoritatively declare the promises I have given you, and thank me and praise me for the victory. Keep doing this until you have a breakthrough."

I thought, *He must be kidding. Here I am, depressed, struggling, exhausted, and frustrated. Okay, maybe I am having a pity party, but I think I have a right to it. All I want to do is crawl into a dark hole somewhere, and God is telling me to proclaim his promises?*

Listlessly, without an ounce of expectation, I picked up my journal and turned to the section where I record the Scriptures and promises that God has impressed on my heart over the years.

At first, I was barely able to whisper. On a scale of one to ten, my enthusiasm level registered minus one hundred, but I kept at it. For several minutes, it seemed like rote. Nothing changed. Discouragement enveloped me like a dark and oppressive cloud.

After about fifteen minutes, I sensed a barely discernible change in my spirit. Beginning as a tiny flicker, a distant light of hope began to penetrate the gloom. It grew a little brighter. Then brighter still. Finally, it seemed to explode with light, and soon I was proclaiming God's Word with authority and conviction. Discouragement broke off me. Completely! The oppressive cloud was gone. Faith and vision were reignited in my heart. Joy soon followed.

Though I had engaged in spiritual warfare in prayer often through the years, I had never encountered such intense discouragement and depression as I did on that particular day. This experience reminded me of the amazing supernatural power available to us when we put on the armour of God and pray, wielding the spiritual weapons he has provided.

One of the most powerful ways of activating your faith is through the Word of God. And remember, "Faith comes by hearing, and hearing by the word of God."[17]

I urge you to write down the promises in God's Word and the spiritual revelation that God gives you. When you face intense opposition, pray and proclaim those promises aggressively and persistently until you have a breakthrough.

The apostle Paul says after you have done all you know to do, stand.[18] Don't be swayed by your emotions. Trust in the Word of God.

Pilots who encounter turbulent weather must learn to trust their instruments, not their feelings. Many pilots have told stories of flying through bad weather, when everything in their senses was telling them different information than what they read on their instruments. Pilots have said they were absolutely certain they were going down and wanted to pull back on the controls (which would have caused them to stall). Others have said they felt sure their aircraft was banking left or right when the instruments said they were climbing straight and true.

Pilots who distrust their instruments and succumb to the overwhelming sense that their aircraft is out of control inevitably crash. It takes unwavering confidence in the instruments, and tremendous strength of will, to refuse to react to their feelings.

God has provided us with his Word as our infallible, unfailing, instrumentation that will guide us through every storm of life. When facing discouragement or obstacles, we are tempted to follow our feelings and human reasoning rather than the Word of God. We are tempted to "take control" and try to fly through the storms on our skills and intellect alone.

Put your faith and confidence in God's Word. If you do, God will navigate you through the storm, and you will see the fulfillment of those things he has promised you.

Run with Peace

Successful long-distance runners demonstrate a graceful ease of posture that propels them to the finish line.

Running the race of purpose also requires a peaceful spiritual posture. If you are stressed out and anxious, striving in your own strength and wisdom, you will find it difficult to persevere.

Running with peace is not a skill developed while lounging by the still waters and green pastures described in the twenty-third psalm—though these seasons of rest are vital times of refreshing on our spiritual journey.

Running with peace is a skill learned during the storms. It is easy to be peaceful when everything is running smoothly. But when storms are swirling around you, it can be a real challenge to rest in God's promises. In those times, I remind myself of the Bible's timeless proven remedy for anxiety: "He who dwells in the shelter of the Most High will rest in the shadow of the Almighty. I will say of the LORD, 'He is my refuge and my fortress, my God, in whom I trust.'"[19]

God's presence is not an escape; it is a bottomless fountain of peace that calms and refreshes us.

I can think of stormy seasons when obstacles and discouragement threatened to overwhelm me. But as I turned my attention away from the storm and hid myself in God's presence, drawing deeply from the fountains of his love and grace, I experienced the reality of this truth: "The peace of God, which transcends all understanding, will guard your hearts and your minds in Christ Jesus."[20]

Sometimes this happened easily. Other times I had to struggle before I experienced the victory of peace. Very few Bible verses tell us to strive about anything. One of those is found in the Book of Hebrews: "Make every effort to enter that rest."[21] Another translation of this verse says, "Strive to enter into that rest."

It may seem like a paradox that we must strive to enter into rest, but this is not referring to a physical, intellectual, or emotional striving; it is a spiritual striving that involves pressing into deeper dependence on our Lord and his promises, until we are truly at rest, trusting in God.

When I experience intense inner stress, sometimes I have to really fight to break through to a place of rest. There's no formula for this; each time, I ask the Holy Spirit to guide my prayers. Sometimes I focus on praise and worship; other times I engage in intense spiritual warfare in prayer; other times I quietly meditate on Scripture; still other times I thank God out loud for his love and provision and for the promises in his Word. Sometimes I sense God directing me to do all these things.

Whether it takes a few minutes or hours, I keep pressing through until the victory of peace comes. It always comes, as long as I don't give up, for God is faithful.

Remember, God is not withholding his peace from you. You have a spiritual enemy, Satan, who will do everything he can to keep you stressed out and anxious. You also have your own humanity to contend with, which easily succumbs to anxiety, but God's Spirit in you is greater and more powerful than these influences.

Whenever you pray, ask the Holy Spirit to lead you. Though at times we easily experience God's peace, at other times, especially in the midst of intense spiritual opposition, we must fight for it.

As you enter into God's rest, you will find it easier to receive his wisdom for dealing with your problems. Empowered by his strength, you will not be crushed by the storms; nor will you give up and quit the race.

When I think of supernatural peace that God has given me during some of the most turbulent storms of my life, I'm reminded of a story I once heard.

An art contest promised a prize to the artist who most effectively depicted the theme "Peace." Numerous artists registered. When the day for judging the entries arrived, the paintings were displayed throughout the gallery. Typical scenes included ducks floating serenely on a quiet pond, palm trees blowing gently in the ocean breeze, moonlight reflecting off a tranquil mountain lake, and other images depicting tranquility.

One painting stood out in stark contrast to the others. At first glance, it seemed anything but peaceful. A violent storm raged over the dark and dreary scene. Trees were bent by a blustering wind. Giant waves threatened to flood a riverbank. In the midst of the chaos was an oak tree. Cradled under its branches was a nest; there, protected under the body of their mother, three baby robins slept peacefully, oblivious to the storm that raged around them. The judges unanimously chose this painting as the winner of the prize.

You, too, can experience the security of those baby robins as they rested peacefully amidst the turbulence. Make God your refuge—and he will give you the grace to remain strong, peaceful, and serene in the midst of raging storms.

Remember the Reason for the Race

As you run your race, you'll encounter many different weather patterns. This is no short stint—it is a long-distance marathon that will take you through a variety of weather systems and diverse landscapes.

Some days will be clear, sunny, and calm; the birds will sing and the flowers will seem as though they are cheering you on your way. Sing along with them, turn your face to the sun, and enjoy this easy, stress-free leg of the race.

Other days will be bleak, dark, and overcast. You may be assaulted by violent storms. Hailstones will leave stinging bruises on your face. Rain will soak through your garments and chill you to the bone. Raging winds will throw obstacles on your path. At times you may feel as though the winds are going to pick you up and crash you against a rock face.

Whatever landscape and weather pattern you are facing at this point on the pathway to making your dreams your destiny, never forget—not even for a moment—the reason for the race. What is that reason? In summarizing the list of characteristics needed to win our race, the Bible concludes, "Let us fix our eyes on Jesus, the author and perfecter of our faith."[22]

Jesus is the reason for the race. *He* is the reason we run. *He* is the reason we passionately pursue the pathway of purpose—to bring glory and honour to him.

The real goal of the race is not to reach our dreams—though that matters to God. He cares deeply about helping us reach our full potential. The goal is not to achieve great feats, though God desires that we impact this world for his glory. The goal is not to be happy, productive, or fulfilled—though these are by-products of obeying God and seeking to fulfill his purpose.

The highest and noblest reason for running the race is to express our love for God. As we draw closer to him and get to know his heart more intimately, we are infused with his passion to touch this hurting world with a message of love, hope, redemption, and healing.

Nothing will blur your vision more than allowing your desire to reach your goals take precedence over your love for God.

Faith sometimes dims because it becomes self-directed rather than fuelled by the desire to honour God. In other words, our dream takes precedence over God himself; our desire to reach our potential becomes more important than our passion for God.

Keep Jesus at the centre of all that you are and all that you do.

If you seek to love him with all of your heart, mind, soul, and strength, you will not be tempted by the endless litany of distractions that will try to steal your affections.

I believe with all my heart that God is leading his children into a brand new season of fruitfulness and victory. Many have carried dreams and promises in their hearts for years, yet they remain unfulfilled. When they look at the reality of their lives, they see no fruit, merely seeds.

But remember, those are no ordinary seeds—they are impregnated by the supernatural life of God. As you continue nurturing them in the fertile soil of your heart, fertilizing them with prayer, the Word of God and obedience, they will gestate and blossom. Remain faithful, and trust your heavenly Father to bring them to maturity in the fullness of his time.

You may feel like a pregnant woman whose baby is overdue—heavy, tired, and longing for the birth. Some days, you wonder if that time will ever come. Some days, you just want it to end. It has been so long, and you yearn for relief from the aching fatigue and heaviness. You may feel you lack the strength to press on to birthing the promises. You may hurt so much that you have stopped caring.

Don't give up on the verge of a miracle! Don't turn back right on the threshold of victory. Remember, it is just prior to the fulfillment of God's promises that Satan launches his most vicious assaults of doubt, fear, and discouragement. It is just when you are about to enter into your own personal Promised Land that the obstacles seem most formidable.

Don't stop now, for your time is coming. God is faithful. He promises that in the same way that rain and snow water the earth, causing it to bud, flourish, and blossom,

> so is my word that goes out from my mouth: It will not return to me empty, but will accomplish what I desire and achieve the purpose for which I sent it. You will go forth in joy and be led forth in peace.[23]

You will birth the divine dreams that God has placed in your heart, if you don't give up. Keep nurturing the seeds of purpose he has planted in your heart, and they will surely blossom.

Whatever God asks you to do, do. Keep putting one foot in front of the other and one day that dream of yours will become your reality and your destiny. And remember, always keep your focus on Jesus, for ultimately, He is the author and finisher of your faith and your dreams.

Faith always wins in the end.

For the vision is yet for an appointed time;
But at the end it will speak, and it will not lie.
Though it tarries, wait for it;
Because it will surely come,
It will not tarry.[24]

Notes

CHAPTER ONE

[1] Matthew 19:26

[2] Matthew 25:14–30

[3] Romans 8:28

[4] Ephesians 3:20

CHAPTER TWO

[1] Genesis 1:27

[2] Romans 1:20

[3] Psalm 19:1

[4] Psalm 8:5

[5] Alma E. Guinness, ed., *ABC's of the Human Body* (New York: Reader's Digest Association, 1987), p. 5

[6] 2 Corinthians 5:17

[7] Romans 8:29; Romans 12:2; 2 Peter 1:4

[8] Philippians 4:13

[9] John 4:34

[10] Os Guinness, *The Call: Finding and Fulfilling the Central Purpose of Your Life* (Nashville: Word Publishing, 1998), p. 3

[11] Psalm 37:4

CHAPTER THREE

1 Romans 8:17
2 Psalm 139:13, 14, 16
3 Jeremiah 29:11
4 John 15:1–8
5 John 3:7
6 Romans 8:16
7 John 15:5
8 John 10:10 (NKJV)
9 Ephesians 2:10 (AMP)
10 Romans 11:29 (AMP)
11 Proverbs 29:18 (AMP)
12 Isaiah 53:4a, 5 (AMP)
13 Romans 8:21
14 Ephesians 2:10
15 2 Corinthians 12:9

CHAPTER FOUR

1 Proverbs 4:23
2 John 7:38
3 John 16:8, 13
4 Galatians 6:7, 8
5 Romans 12:2
6 Psalm 1:1–3
7 John 15:5–7
8 James 1:21
9 John 8:32
10 Hebrews 4:12
11 Philippians 4:6, 7
12 Isaiah 40:31 (NKJV)
13 John 10:4
14 John 16:13, 14
15 1 Kings 19:12b (NKJV)
16 Proverbs 23:7 (NKJV)
17 2 Corinthians 10:5b
18 Philippians 4:8

CHAPTER FIVE

1 Brent Curtis and John Eldredge, *The Sacred Romance* (Nashville: Thomas Nelson, 1997), p. 116

2 John 10:10

3 1 John 3:8

4 Luke 4:18 (NKJV)

5 Romans 12:2

6 Psalm 66:10

7 John 12:24

8 Proverbs 17:3

9 Hebrews 6:12

10 Proverbs 3:5, 6

11 Ephesians 2:10

CHAPTER SIX

1 2 Kings 2:10–14

2 Ecclesiastes 3:1

3 Isaiah 43:18, 19

4 Philippians 3:13, 14

5 Christopher Petersen, "Optimism and Bypass Surgery," *Learned Helplessness: A Theory for the Age of Personal Control* (New York: Oxford Univ. Press, 1993), p. 2

6 John 14:12

7 Ephesians 3:20

8 Genesis 18:14

CHAPTER SEVEN

1 Psalm 119:105

2 Ephesians 1:17, 18 (NKJV)

3 Genesis 12:1–6; 17:1–8

4 Genesis 15:1–6

5 1 Corinthians 4:2

6 Luke 16:10 (NKJV)

7 Genesis 16

8 Genesis 21:1–6

[9] Genesis 22:12

[10] 1 Samuel 16:6

[11] 1 Samuel 16:7

[12] Luke 1:38

[13] Psalm 138:2

[14] 1 Peter 1:25

[15] John 1:14

[16] John 17:17

[17] Proverbs 20:27 (NKJV)

[18] Romans 8:16

[19] Philippians 4:7

[20] Romans 8:14

[21] 1 Corinthians 10:31

[22] Proverbs 11:14

[23] Philippians 3:8

[24] Proverbs 3:5, 6

[25] Psalm 25:4, 5

CHAPTER EIGHT

[1] Psalm 37:4

[2] Psalm 40:8

[3] John Ortberg, *If You Want to Walk on Water You've Got to Get out of the Boat* (Grand Rapids: Zondervan, 2001), p. 58

[4] 1 Peter 4:10 (AMP)

[5] Rick Warren, *The Purpose Driven Life* (Grand Rapids: Zondervan, 2002), p. 251

[6] Colossians 3:17

CHAPTER NINE

[1] Psalm 32:8

[2] Proverbs 16:9

[3] Habakkuk 2:2 (NKJV)

[4] Stephen R. Covey, *First Things First* (New York: Simon & Schuster, 1994), p. 107

[5] George Barna, *The Power of Vision* (Ventura: Regal Books, 1992), pp. 39, 46

6 James 2:17

7 Jack Canfield, Mark Victor Hansen, Les Hewitt, *The Power of Focus* (Deerfield Beach: Health Communications Inc., 2000), pp. 61–62

8 Hebrews 11:1 (NKJV)

9 Proverbs 16:3

CHAPTER TEN

1 Cheryl Richardson, *Stand Up for Your Life* (New York: The Free Press, 2002), p. 10

2 John 8:32

3 Philippians 4:13

4 1 Corinthians 1:30; 2 Corinthians 5:21

5 Psalm 32:8

6 Isaiah 55:9

7 Psalm 25:14 (AMP)

8 Deuteronomy 28:1a, 2

9 Joshua 1:7

10 Joshua 7:9b

11 Joshua 7:10, 11

12 Daniel 11:32 (AMP)

CHAPTER ELEVEN

1 1 Timothy 4:14

2 2 Timothy 1:6, 7

3 Proverbs 29:25; Proverbs 14:27

4 2 Corinthians 1:20

5 1 John 4:16b, 18

6 Ephesians 3:17–19

7 James 2:17

8 2 Corinthians 12:9

9 Ephesians 6:10, 11, 14–18

10 Joshua 3:13

11 Romans 1:17; Galatians 3:11; Hebrews 10:38

12 Gregg Levoy, *Callings: Finding and Following an Authentic Life* (New York: Harmony Books, 1997), p. 250

[13] Isaiah 54:2, 3a

CHAPTER TWELVE
[1] Hebrews 12:1, 2a (NKJV)
[2] Hebrews 12:1b (NKJV)
[3] Joshua 1:4
[4] 1 Samuel 30:6 (KJV)
[5] 1 Timothy 1:18 (NKJV)
[6] Psalm 36:5
[7] Colossians 1:29
[8] Isaiah 30:18d
[9] Hebrews 12:1
[10] Ephesians 5:18
[11] Matthew 25:21
[12] Hebrews 6:11, 12
[13] James 1:2–4
[14] Hebrews 11:6
[15] Ephesians 6:16
[16] Ephesians 6:17
[17] Romans 10:17 (NKJV)
[18] Ephesians 6:13
[19] Psalm 91:1, 2
[20] Philippians 4:7
[21] Hebrews 4:11
[22] Hebrews 12:2
[23] Isaiah 55:11, 12
[24] Habakkuk 2:3 (NKJV)

Peace with God

After reading this book, I hope you have come to understand how deeply God loves you and how much he desires to help you understand and fulfill your purpose.

Your potential can never be realized, however, if you are disconnected from your spiritual source.

If you have not yet made peace with God, you can do that today. You can experience the reality of God's presence. You can have the inner assurance that God hears your prayers.

According to the Bible, every one of us has sinned. The Bible says, "For all have sinned and fall short of the glory of God." But the very next verse promises that we can be "justified freely by his grace through the redemption that came by Christ Jesus."[1]

Sin separates us from God's presence, peace, and power in this life. And it prevents us from entering the sacred holiness of heaven in eternity. Jesus Christ, God's Son, died on the cross to pay the penalty for our sins. He was resurrected from death and is alive today. He comes to dwell in us by his Holy Spirit when we receive his gift of forgiveness.

When we receive Jesus Christ as our Saviour and Lord, our spirits are awakened to knowledge of God. Rather than just knowing about God or believing in the existence of God, we truly know him in our newly born spirits. As the Bible says, "The Spirit himself testifies with our spirit that we are God's children."[2]

God promises a new beginning to everyone who becomes his child. The Message paraphrase of the Bible says that

> anyone united with the Messiah gets a fresh start, is created new. The old life is gone; a new life burgeons! Look at it! All this comes from the God who settled the relationship between us and him.[3]

Through Jesus Christ you can experience peace that endures, grace that empowers, love that heals, and faith that spurs you forward into your destiny.

Salvation is a free gift. You cannot earn it; you can only receive it by faith. Jesus Christ is waiting for an invitation to come into your life and recreate you into the person you were destined to be. All you need to do is invite him in by faith. Acknowledge your sin, admit your need for him, and ask him to come into your heart and become your personal Saviour and Lord. It doesn't matter exactly what words you use. Following is a suggested guideline for prayer:

Dear Lord Jesus,

I know I am a sinner and need your forgiveness. I believe that you are the Son of God and that you died on the cross to pay the penalty for my sins. I believe that you rose from the dead and that you are alive today. I ask you to forgive me of my sins, of going my own way, of trying to live life without you. I ask you to come into my heart and become my Saviour and Lord. Please help me to grow in my relationship with you. Help me to understand and fulfill the unique purpose you planned for my life. Thank you for the gift of eternal life, and thank you for the gift of your Holy Spirit, who has now come to live in me. In Jesus' name, Amen.

If you prayed this prayer sincerely from your heart, you are now God's child. He accepts you just the way you are. You are forgiven, cleansed, and given a fresh start. The barrier separating you from God's love and presence has been removed, for Jesus has reconciled you to your heavenly Father.

If you have just made a commitment to Christ and would like me to e-mail you a free e-book to help you grow in your faith, e-mail faith@lifetoolsforwomen.com with your request.

Welcome to the family of God!

---

[1] Romans 3:23, 24

[2] Romans 8:16

[3] 2 Corinthians 5:17, 18 (THE MESSAGE)